YOUR
OWNERSHIP
JOURNEY

12 SECRETS FOR PERSONAL
AND BUSINESS SUCCESS

BRUCE WERNER
STRATEGIC ADVISOR TO PRIVATE BUSINESSES

INDIE BOOKS
INTERNATIONAL

No part of this publication may be reproduced or distributed in any form or by any means, without the prior permission of the publisher. Requests for permission should be directed to permissions@indiebooksintl.com, or mailed to Permissions, Indie Books International, 2424 Vista Way, Suite 316, Oceanside, CA 92054.

The views and opinions in this book are those of the author at the time of writing this book, and do not reflect the opinions of Indie Books International or its editors.

Neither the publisher nor the author is engaged in rendering legal or other professional services through this book. If expert assistance is required, the services of appropriate professionals should be sought. The publisher and the author shall have neither liability nor responsibility to any person or entity with respect to any loss or damage caused directly or indirectly by the information in this publication.

Good Housekeeping Seal. The "Good Housekeeping Seal", a limited warranty program that is popularly known as the "Good Housekeeping Seal of Approval", is a registered trademark of Good Housekeeping magazine. The publisher is Hearst Magazines. The use in the text is a metaphor, not meant to imply endorsement.

EOS. Entrepreneurial Operating System®, or EOS®, is a registered trademark of EOS Worldwide. The use in this book is not an endorsement, but for informational purposes only.

Vistage. Vistage® is a registered trademark of Vistage International. The use in this book is not an endorsement, but for informational purposes only.

YPO. YPO®, which stands for Young President's Organization, is a registered trademark of YPO, INC. The use in this book is not an endorsement, but for informational purposes only.

All stories and case studies in this book are based on true stories, but names and some details have been changed to protect confidentiality. These stories are included for educational purposes, to help business leaders better understand the points that are being made.

ISBN 13: 978-1-952233-97-5
Library of Congress Control Number: 2022901665

Designed by Bill Ramsey

INDIE BOOKS INTERNATIONAL®, INC.
2424 VISTA WAY, SUITE 316
OCEANSIDE, CA 92054
www.indiebooksintl.com

Contents

Preface

Whether you are a veteran, novice, aspiring business owner, or you operate a private or family business, I know you'll find some nuggets of gold as you read through the pages of this book. The unveiled process—through twelve secrets—will apply to any owner, plus there is a chapter devoted to the specific needs of family businesses.

I'd like you to think about two key concepts as you learn the secrets:

- Clarify your life goals—financial security, family harmony, enjoyment of time well spent, etc. You can make more money, but you can't make more time.
- Develop a business strategy so the business is managed to enable you to achieve your life goals— never forgetting that the business is an asset.

On my first day of college, I walked into the lecture hall, anxiously waiting for the professor. In comes Prof. P. K. Wright, inspiring to all in his Savile Row suit and proper British accent. He started by telling a story.

"You are going to spend four years studying many things. Most of it you will never use. However, we know you will use about 10 percent of what you learn. The problem is we don't know which 10 percent it is, so you have to study all of it."

This book is something like that. You have built a good business and want to make it better. You know or have a sense of much of what is in this book. The trick is to find the 10 percent that moves your needle.

Bruce Werner
Chicago
September 2021

Why The Ownership Journey Is A Rocky Road

What to do when your house catches fire, when the levee breaks, or when you are buried alive?

Yes, it is a dangerous world out there. Despite the dramatic leaps we have taken in technology, medicine, and global awareness, danger still lurks beneath the surface, around the corner, and behind the door.

That's the view of a great book that has been a twenty-year international bestseller: *The Worst-Case Scenario Survival Handbook.*[1] The guide offers techniques, advice, and info that could save your life, limbs, and loved ones. Because it's a dangerous world out there.

I feel the same about the lurking dangers of owning a business. I intend to give business owners valuable information so they can survive the worst-case scenarios the world can throw at them.

The Ownership Journey Is A Rocky Road

If you have ever been to an Irish pub, you probably have heard the nineteenth-century standard of Irish folk music, "Rocky Road To Dublin." The song describes the trials, troubles, and travails that the protagonist encounters on his travels. At the beginning of the song, the story's protagonist states that he is off to seek his fortune. Along the way, he encounters many adventures and troubles.

If you are on the ownership journey, you know about troubles.

Why can the ownership journey be a rocky road? In a nutshell, it's because nobody is there to guide you, tell you when you need to make a decision, or what's the question you're trying to answer. The search for answers separates the leaders from the managers and the managers from the followers.

A catchphrase I often use is this: It's not about finding the right answers in life. It's about asking the right questions. If you don't ask the right question, you'll never get the right answer. This is true as a business owner, and it's also true as a consultant. I press clients because after I ask a number of questions, when I finally ask the right ones, they say, "Yeah, that's what I really meant."

Those who don't have the wherewithal to understand when a decision needs to be made probably shouldn't be the boss. That might sound harsh, but it's the truth—because defining the decision to be made and understanding when the decision has to be made really determines the outcome. A too-narrow definition, made so painful decisions can be avoided, means the real issue is being avoided.

Consider the most important question: "Why are you in business?" Most owners don't stop to dissect that question into its parts. Many people do not distinguish between "Who do you want to be?" from "What do you want to do?" What this is asking is:

- What are your life goals, and how does the business help you to achieve those goals: financial security, happiness, family harmony, enjoyment of time well spent? You can make more money, but you can't make more time.
- How does your business strategy enable you to achieve your life goals? The business is an asset, and it should be used to help you achieve your life goals.

From that perspective, it is easier to define a process to help owners achieve their life and business goals. Where they are today is Point A. Where they want to get to is Point B. Once the two endpoints are defined, it is more straightforward to construct a road from A to B. Success is about perseverance and adapting to changes beyond your control.

The discipline of execution is the responsibility of leadership, with board oversight. If there is no functioning board, as is often the case with private companies, then it is a matter of what the owners will accept.

A Worst-Case Scenario For A Private Company

When you see a company get into trouble, it is usually because management failed to adjust to market conditions. This is often because change is hard, uncomfortable, or inconvenient to their lifestyle. If the owners tolerate it, then it is fine.

In a recent conversation with the chairperson of a $750 million family business, she expressed her frustration that the company has been losing money for years and couldn't get the management team to right-size the business. The market had shrunk due to COVID-19, and the business could only support about $300 million in revenue. Too many vested interests were being protected.

Once I explained the difference between an ownership strategy and business strategy, a lightbulb went on. Ownership strategy defines what the owners want from the asset they own. A business strategy is what you do to get there. She realized she was letting the highly paid management team drive the ownership strategy. That was fine with them since it was not their money being burned, and they did not want to execute the painful staff reductions needed to make the company solvent.

The Lazy Path To A Lifestyle Business

Another issue is when owners get too comfortable and start to focus on having a lifestyle business. This is what blue water sailors call "harbor fever." They want to avoid potential storms, so they stay in the harbor. Owners are not accountable for their behavior to anyone but themselves. Many businesses get in trouble because things are allowed to slide until an outside force steps in to stop them. And that usually happens when they get in trouble with the bank; they then fix their business, going through a brutally painful and avoidable process.

The bottom line here is that while it's great to be a private company owner, there's this unspoken responsibility when it comes to self-discipline. When owners get in trouble, it's because they got too comfortable with the status quo, failed to adapt to changing market conditions—and typically waited too long to act.

Leadership, Decisiveness, And Corporate Rejuvenation

An adage says that private company owners can do whatever they want, so long as they pay their taxes and their bank is happy. As the owners move through the decades of life, material success tends to damper commercial drive, and people become increasingly comfortable with the status quo. This is one reason why many private companies tend to become lifestyle businesses, and young people create start-ups.

Choosing the path forward, dynamic growth versus comfortable continuity, is a test of ownership, not management. If the ownership likes things the way they are, management will follow their lead. If the ownership and management are the same individuals, they may not even realize their decision since no one is challenging their perspective.

Here are two examples of situations that demonstrate the point:

Rejuvenation: It is easy for owners to get disinterested, bored, or somewhat lazy as time marches on. For owners in their sixties and seventies, it can be difficult to fix a business they have run a certain way for twenty to thirty years. If the company gets into trouble, it almost always needs an external actor to drive substantial change. Hence the adage about taxes and the bank.

In a recent situation, a seventy-year-old family business had missed the window to move online, and its revenue fell in half. Now in semi-retirement, the owner realized his mistake yet knew he didn't have what was needed to fix it himself. To his credit, he hired an outside CEO from the digital world to lead the transition. He also rebooted his board of advisors to provide oversight and keep things fresh. While he had made a serious mistake, he recognized his mistake and acted while there was enough time to avoid calamity.

Stasis. Opposing this decisiveness is a second-generation family business that had decades of success but was now deadlocked on what to do next. One set of cousins, the three sisters that were passive owners, wanted to sell their interests to the brother and sister who ran the business. The operating cousins liked things the way they "used to be" before the digital age. The company was healthy, debt-free, and had piles of cash. But competitive pressures were building as the competition went digital. What was also true was that the business could double in size and become quite exciting for everyone if someone would lead the way forward. No one wanted to jeopardize personal relationships, even though it created substantial unhappiness for everyone.

This company had a board of directors comprised of the five cousins but lacked effective governance mechanisms. While the company was profitable, the dividend policy was meager, such that the returns were well below market. This caused frustration with the passive owners who viewed the business as an investment, more than a family legacy to protect. The outside cousins recognized that their investment could grow significantly if a new CEO stepped in to drive growth. No one was against that, and all were in favor of the change, but, also, no one was pushing to make it happen.

There was no way to break a tie vote, and the outside cousins were not allowed to sell their interests to anyone but the inside cousins. The inside cousins could sit on their hands if they wanted. Over the years, the frustration built up, and the situation became tense.

Leadership is about recognizing that a decision needs to be made and making it before it is too late. Governance defines how the decision gets made. That is true no matter how large or small the business may be.

In the first situation, decision-making was streamlined because only one vote mattered. The second situation proves that when there are multiple owners, governing the business is a job above and beyond running the business.

These situations provide contrast to highlight what is needed to keep a private business vibrant. The hardest part of initiating corporate rejuvenation is deciding to make a big decision.

Make Decisions Faster Than The River Runs

When I went to summer camp as a child, I was taught to row a canoe on a river. The secret was to always paddle faster than the river was running. If you are faster than the river, you can control where the canoe goes. If not, you will end up on the rocks.

Similarly, in business, if you make decisions faster than the pace of change, you can control your destiny by adjusting course based on changing circumstances. If you slow down to enjoy the comforts of success, you may also end up on the rocks.

This is the story of how my family's business avoided the rocks. In the 1970s, the Werner Co. had come a long way since Richard D. Werner founded the company in 1922.

The company became a leader in plastics extrusion during World War II restrictions on civilian metal usage. After the war, Werner started working with aluminum and developed an emphasis on producing aluminum ladders. The main factory was in Greenville, Pennsylvania, and there was an assembly plant by O'Hare Airport in Chicago. The Chicago plant was built to service major retail customers: Montgomery Ward and several major wholesale hardware distributors.

But, in the 1970s, the second generation, three brothers and a cousin, were college-educated engineers coming into their most productive professional years looking to secure their futures. After all, they needed to provide for the third generation, which they hoped would succeed them in the family business.

Werner Co. faced a tough decision on its ownership journey. It needed to assess its leadership if it was to continue to grow and be positioned for generational succession.

This is a cautionary tale about the possible consequences of not making business decisions at all—a decision in itself.

Werner Co. had established itself as a reliable supplier with competitive product and manufacturing technology. These advantages, along with novel marketing and great customer service, drove continued growth. Part of the strategy was to assure that customers never needed to buy niche products elsewhere, which is why Werner Co. had a full catalog of industrial, commercial, and residential products.

But production capacity was limited to two small extrusion presses. Due to extrusion capacity limits, Werner Co. reluctantly began to outsource its extrusions. The company disliked doing so due to significant cost penalties and lost productivity.

Being a private company, Werner Co. had limited access to capital, and a new extrusion facility would cost tens of millions of dollars. If the company was going to make this investment, it needed new technology, which would leapfrog the competition by a generation. The company knew the unique technical features it wanted, but no one was building that sophisticated equipment. So, Werner Co. had to find an equipment builder capable and willing to do so, which it did to get the productivity required.

Richard D. Werner had retired some years earlier but was still in charge of the company. His younger brother, Leo, was the president and had helped to professionalize the business. While the founder was a true risk-taker, at this point, his younger brother, a widower, had become much more conservative. He was at the end of his career, the business had grown substantially, and he did not want to make a strategic mistake. So, he avoided making decisions. The idea of betting the company on a new investment with unproven technology was not something he could condone.

So, this became a generational conflict, as often happens in family businesses. The younger generation wanted to drive growth, and the older generation was becoming more risk-averse. The four second-generation men knew that customers would go elsewhere if they did not add capacity soon, and growth would be stunted. It would personally impact them. They were young, smart, aggressive, and confident that they could do great things with the business.

The president stalled making a business decision for several years until it became clear he was avoiding the issue. So, on a bright day in May 1977 in Manhattan, following the weekend that the second grandchild was married, the four second-generation leaders met with the founder.

Fortunately, the founder, who built the business through wars and depressions, understood the need to make timely decisions. He realized that the right thing to do for the company was to put the customers first and satisfy demand. He had faith in his nephews, as he had seen them work together for over twenty years. He realized that it was time for his younger brother to step aside and let the next generation lead. The owner turned over control to the younger generation and authorized the expansion.

The increased capacity was built using proprietary new technology that raised the bar on quality and productivity. The company did this again in 1986. These decisions laid the foundation for the Werner Co. you see today.

No Business Decision Is
A Bad Business Decision

This Werner Co. story demonstrates that avoiding making business decisions, especially tough ones, is the same as making a decision. This is too easy in family businesses where decisions are hard or emotionally difficult. This is one of the burdens of ownership.

Successful leaders understand this and do not vacillate when a decision needs to be made. They take the time to gather the information needed to be fully informed and talk to all stakeholders to get buy-in. But the challenge of leadership is that no one tells you when you need to make a decision or what the right answer is. You need to figure out the answers to those questions, often alone.

What you need to know is that on this rocky road, ownership strategy decisions come first. That will be examined in the next chapter.

Your Ownership Journey

Secret #1. Why The Ownership Journey Is A Rocky Road

» It's not about finding the right answers in life. It's about asking the right questions.

» While most of your time is spent working *in* the business, the high-impact decisions you will make pertain to working *on* the business.

» Ownership strategy defines what the owners want from the asset they own. A business strategy is what you do to get there.

» Private company owners can do whatever they want, so long as they pay their taxes and their bank is happy.

» When you see a company get into trouble, it is usually because management failed to adjust to market conditions.

» It is easy for owners to get too comfortable as time marches on.

Ownership Strategy Comes First

In 1860, Milton Bradley, a publisher and game pioneer, invented a classic board game known today as The Game of Life. You probably played it as a child. In the game, players work their way through various paths in life, with the goal, of course, to win the game of life.

That phrase "the game of life" is apt for business owners as well. Why else are you working so hard?

To win the game of life, you need an ownership strategy that positions you, as an individual, where you want to be when you get to the fourth quarter of life. This is more than just a business strategy.

To Win The Game Of Business, You Need An Ownership Strategy

After working with business owners for many years, I've concluded that most business owners don't understand the need to have an ownership strategy that's separate from their business strategy.

This involves focusing on many things: their age, where they are in life and how that influences their point of view, the stage of the business, and their perceived wisdom at dealing with challenges. Their risk tolerance, ability to execute, and ability to deal with adversity are also important to consider.

It all starts with a basic question: "Why are you in business?"
Most owners don't stop to dissect the question into its parts.
What the question is asking is:

- What are your life goals—financial security, happiness, family harmony, enjoyment of time well spent—and how does the business help you achieve them? You can make more money, but you can't make more time.
- How does your business strategy enable you to achieve your life goals? The business is an asset, and it should be used to help you achieve your life goals.

From that perspective, it is easier to define a process to help owners achieve their life and business goals. Where they are today is Point A. Where they want to get is Point B. Once the two endpoints are defined, it is more straightforward to construct a road from A to B. Success is about perseverance and adapting to changes beyond your control.

Consider The Tale Of Acme Widgets

Acme Widgets Inc. was a second-generation family business that had struggled for some years. (Based on a true story, but details have been changed to protect confidentiality.) The CEO, Andrew Acme, decided it was time to work smarter, not harder. He was approaching fifty and knew he did not want to keep working this hard indefinitely. When I asked him what his ownership strategy was, at first, he didn't understand. When we started to peel back the issues, things came into focus for him. He had specific financial goals in mind but never put them on paper before.

When Mr. Acme called me in, we flushed out what Acme Widgets would need to look like for him to retire by age fifty-eight. We then built an EBITDA (Earnings Before Interest, Taxes, Depreciation, and Amortization) bridge of how Acme Widgets was going to get from here to there, with high-level assumptions. You can see what it looks like below.

We then dug one level deeper to substantiate the major assumptions. We ran a few market tests on new products and channels to confirm the strategy. It is now seven years later, and Acme has surpassed these goals.

This is a classic example of starting with the answer and working backwards to where you are today. The chart below shows you the Acme Widget numbers.

ACME WIDGETS

EBITDA	2019	2020	2021	2022	2023
Base Line					
Current Business-Domestic	$7,600,000	$10,000,000	$10,800,000	$12,050,000	$14,050,000
Current Business-Catalog	$2,900,000	$3,800,000	$4,250,000	$4,750,000	$5,750,000
Current Business-Custom	$1,700,000	$2,537,000	$2,537,000	$2,537,000	$3,287,000
Incremental Change					
New Product Lines-Domestic		$750,000	$1,250,000	$2,000,000	$3,000,000
New Product Lines-Catalog			$500,000	$1,000,000	$1,350,000
New Product Lines-Custom				$750,000	$1,250,000
Acquisitions			$4,000,000	$5,500,000	$6,500,000
Overseas Revenue				$500,000	$100,000
Total Sales	$12,200,00	$17,087,000	$23,337,000	$29,087,000	$35,287,000
EBIDTA	$380,000	$1,196,090	$2,800,440	$4,653,920	$6,351,660
% Gross Margin	30%	32%	35%	38%	40%
% Expense: Revenue	27.0%	25.0%	23.0%	22.0%	22.0%
% EBITDA: Revenue	3.0%	7.0%	12.0%	16.0%	18.0%

So how do you win the game of life? As the saying goes, no one died wishing they had spent more time at the office. At the end of life, a person thinks about what is important, whether they lived a good life, how they will be remembered, and if they're happy.

While many of those subjects are outside the scope of this book, the question of happiness is not. So, what is happiness?

What Is Happiness?

Most people don't start a business to find happiness. But if they have success, they start to think about more than just making money. As we age, our priorities change due to what life hands us along the way. At some point, when you have some financial security and have survived a few challenges, you start to think about happiness.

As a young adult, I was told that happiness occurs when you accept your situation in life, whatever that may be.

As we age, we also tend to think about bigger issues, the proverbial "meaning of life" issues. Meaning is different from happiness as well. It has more to do with purpose and the feelings that occur when one positively impacts the world around them.

Here is what author Darrin McMahon writes about the origins and root words of the word happiness:

It is a striking fact that in every Indo-European language, without exception, going all the way back to ancient Greek, the word for happiness is a cognate with the word for luck. Hap is the Old Norse and Old English root of happiness, and it just means luck or chance, as did the Old French heur, giving us bonheur, good fortune or happiness. German gives us the word Gluck, which to this day means both happiness and chance.[2]

There is some science to happiness. It is a state of being, not a trait, so it may change over time. It comes and goes. It is different from the more intense feelings of bliss, joy, ecstasy, or other such feelings.

Happiness is different from pleasure. The former is a state of being, while the latter is more sensory-based and likely to be fleeting. Pursuing pleasure does not always lead to happiness; for the same reason, there is often declining marginal pleasure from acquiring material possessions. (How many Ferraris do you really need? How much lobster and caviar can you eat?)

Some portion of our happiness is genetic. Scientists estimate that genetics is 10 to 50 percent of the reason one may or may not be happy.[3]

We instinctively know that financial security, good health, vibrant relationships, and positive emotions contribute to happiness. As I look at friends and family who appear happy, those with good relationships tend to stick out as happy, and those with poor relationships tend not to be in the happy crowd.

So why talk about happiness in a book about your owner-ship journey? At some point, it is just work, and successful owners want more from life than a job and a paycheck. They want to do something with their lives: something with meaning and impact, creating a legacy to be proud of. This is the human condition for true entrepreneurs and owners.

If you are successful, happiness is where you want to arrive.

How Age And Environment Constrain Options

The more private companies I work with, the more I wonder how owners make their decisions— not just the final answer, but how they dissect the situation, assess risks and proba-bilities, adjust for personalities, and then decide when they are ready. If you don't understand an owner's perspective with sufficient nuance, some of their decisions will always remain perplexing.

The same person could act differently in different situations. One conclusion is to reaffirm Miles' Law: "Where you stand depends on where you sit."

Perhaps it is not about the decision-making but the stage they are at that drives their choices. When you adjust for the stage of the business, the maturity of the decision-maker, and their level of wisdom, then it is easier to understand things that, at first, don't appear logical.

The three major factors the decision-maker needs to acknowledge are the stage of the business, the age of the decision-maker, and finally, the evolution of their wisdom and judgment.

The stage of the business frames the opportunities and constraints. The age of the decision-maker is a metric of their risk tolerance, agility, and aggressiveness. Wisdom and judgment fall along a spectrum from youth to old age. While there is no metric to measure wisdom, time has shown that it can be identified with a clear eye.

Two well-informed people, given the same business stage and age, are likely to make different decisions based on their wisdom and judgment. There are many writings on these topics, so let's understand what is already known to help inform future decision-making.

Business Lifecycle

The business lifecycle consists of five phases: launch, growth, shake-out, maturity, and decline. It is easy to use revenue, profits, and cash flow to mark the transition between the phases.

The launch phase is associated with starting a new business: no revenue, a lot of costs, high risk, and uncertainty. If the business gets traction, it moves to the growth phase. This is the exciting part of the lifecycle and what Silicon Valley made famous in its early days.

The shake-out phase is like being a teenager. It is not as much fun as being a kid; things start to go wrong sometimes and getting into trouble can change the course of your life. This means sales growth starts to slow, competition hurts profit margins, more investment is needed, and cash flow needs attention.

A business in its maturity is stabilized, generating cash flow, and may have a secure competitive position. However, it likely needs to evolve before it loses its competitive advantage. Productive reinvention is rewarded. Without it, decline sets in.

The decline phase marks the end of the productive years of the business. It will likely be sold or cease operations. The decline is always easier to see in hindsight and often missed while there is still time to fix the business.

Human Maturity Process

Carl Jung, the famous psychologist, was rumored to say he "would take no patient under the age of forty since they are still children." When I was young, I thought I could think my way out of challenges and that my elders were holding me back. As I aged, I realized how right Jung was and how wrong I was.

A decision-maker's maturity and life experiences influence how they evaluate situations, identify and judge risks, and adapt accordingly.

My observation that these archetypes coincide with the decades of life is not a fluke. Psychologists, such as Erik H. Erikson, have researched and documented this phenomenon.[4] Our brains grow and evolve with time. Cells used more live longer. Cells not used tend to die.

Children and teenagers are curious since their brains develop via trial and error. Learning creates the circuits that allow the person to evolve. Neuron connections change as the brain becomes more active; over time, more connections are made. Brain scans can see which parts of the brain are more activated at different ages.

As we age, the circuits become substantially complete, and the learning rate may slow or become more specialized. This is a biological function. Older brains are less able to multitask and remember details, but they do well using established knowledge to make decisions.

Developing Wisdom

When we think about parents and friends in their eighth and ninth decade of life, we tend to think about wisdom or frailty. Knowledge means you know something (e.g., memorizing facts and figures). Wisdom is defined as having experience and knowledge, and the the ability to know when and how to apply that experience and knowledge (e.g., when to not say something).

Werner Wisdom

As the adage says: "You are truly educated when you understand how little you know."

Another definition of wisdom uses a collection of adjectives to define something which, frankly, scientists and doctors have yet to define easily: understanding, prudence, discernment, foresight, control, flexibility, and persistence.

Wisdom is a business issue since it has the most impact in uncertain, variable, and risky situations. If you can solve a problem with a spreadsheet, then it is an easy problem to solve. When there is no one to ask for help, then wisdom is invaluable.

How We Make Decisions

So, what can we do to better control our fate?

- Understand that biology and environment influence our decisions
- Get help to hedge these biases (hence why companies have boards and hire consultants)
- Seek wisdom to make better decisions to get better outcomes

Most people work to provide for their families, but business owners are different. They took the risk to get started, with the expectation of being rewarded for the risk. They expect more from life than just a paycheck. They are also willing to sacrifice more and work harder and longer to get what they want from life.

Werner Wisdom

As the saying goes: "It is better to be lucky than good."

The next secret to examine on the journey is how business strategy drives objectives and tactics.

Your Ownership Journey

Secret #2. Ownership Strategy Comes First

» Consider how owning a business will help you win the game of life.

» The business is an asset, and it should be used to help you achieve your life goals.

» Success is about perseverance and adapting to changes beyond your control.

» Wisdom is a business issue since it has the most impact in uncertain, variable, and risky situations.

» Pursuing pleasure does not always lead to happiness; for the same reason, there is often declining marginal pleasure from acquiring material possessions.

Get The Business Strategy Right, Then Drive

Remember math word problems back in grade school? These word problems were about mathematical modeling.

A simple exercise: Patty had six dollars, then spent four dollars. How much does she have now?

Examples of math word problems can be found dating back to Babylonian times. Most ancient Babylonian problems are couched in a language of measurement of everyday objects and activities.[5]

Another exercise: Belteshazzar had six shekels, then spent four shekels. How much does he have now?

When I build a business strategy, I start with learning what owners want. That turns into a mathematical modeling word problem.

Getting The Business Strategy Math Right

Let's say Jordan owns a $25 million revenue business and wants to get to $100 million. His financial planner has told him if he sells a $100 million business he will have financial security and be able to do the things he wants when he retires.

His magic number is $25 million in the bank since he intends to collect art and buy a few houses and boats. He thinks he can make this happen and is willing to take the risk to get there.

His business produces 8 percent EBITDA, and businesses in his industry trade at five to six times EBITDA. So, if he sells a $100 million business, after taxes and expenses, he should be able to net about $25 million to $30 million, assuming he is debt-free. To build the business strategy, we work backwards, knowing he needs to get to $100 million in revenue to achieve his ownership goal.

One of the things we can't change is the industry growth rate. If an owner needs to grow at 15 percent a year to get to $50 million revenue, and the industry is growing at 7 percent a year, there is a gap. That owner's choices are inventing something hot, growing faster (not a good plan), or acquiring. Let's say the owner decides he can grow 7 percent organically and buy other businesses that also have that 7 percent growth rate a year, then together he can hit the $50 million goal in five years.

That being decided, the owner needs to figure out how he grows his business 7 percent a year—does he need more factories, more staff, more salespeople? That's running a business. At the same time, the owner needs to build an acquisition team to find targets, buy them, integrate them, and have them be successful.

Top-Down And Bottom-Up

Strategy is done top-down; implementation is done bottom-up.

You build a business strategy from the top, working down, layer by layer. You keep peeling back until you have it figured out—and then it's time to act, implementing the plan from the bottom up. It is a virtuous loop if done properly. If you have the right plan and execute the details properly, you should get the right results. Lots of companies have great ideas, but if they can't execute, it doesn't matter.

Understanding Your Competitive Model

Strategy was once defined as trying to gain an unfair advantage in the marketplace. Michael Porter published a book in 1980 that reframed the discussion on competitive strategy.[6] Businesses compete to produce superior returns for the investors. These returns depend on the industry and how a business positions itself within that industry.

Every industry has a natural growth rate (e.g., software {Google} vs. grocery {Safeway}) and a natural level of profitability (e.g., online advertising vs. food). Once you pick your industry, the rules of competition are pretty much set. But you can control how you position your business within that industry, and that part of strategy is controllable.

Porter defined five forces in strategy development:

- Rivalry among competitors
- Bargaining power of suppliers

- Bargaining power of customers
- Threats from new entrants
- Threats from substitute products/services

Your ability to gain an unfair advantage depends on understanding these five forces and making decisions to do better than your competition overall within your market.

Porter's Model Of Competition

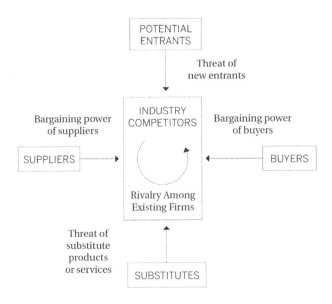

From this point, he then defined the five basic competitive strategies for a business. While these are generic, they are the jumping-off point for developing a strategy for your business.

Porter's Definition Of The Three Basic Competitive Strategies

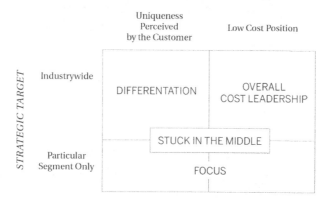

What you don't want to be is "stuck in the middle." That means you are roadkill waiting to happen since you have no advantage over your competition. You need to have a sustainable long-term competitive advantage if your business is to survive and prosper.

From this work, the phrase "value proposition" became popular. But what does this phrase mean? Simply put: Know who your customers are, deeply understand their needs, and price your offering at a price your customers consider to be at least fair value to them. This process will force you to think about how to grow your business and increase your profitability.

Structure Follows Strategy

Once you have developed a competitive strategy based on your industry that provides you with a long-term competitive advantage, how do you organize your business to execute that strategy?

The seminal work on industrial organization was written by Alfred Chandler in 1962.[7] He was the first to tie together business strategy, organizational structure, market dynamics, and entrepreneurship. His famous quote is "Structure follows strategy," meaning the organization's structure depends on its business strategy.

His research focused on American industry from 1850 to about 1920. This research categorized businesses and their evolution. He defined four stages of industrial development and provided specific case studies to prove his points. While Adam Smith described the invisible hand, Chandler defined the visible hand as "a company's total control of the entire process from raw materials to the final product."

Until 1850, American businesses were small enterprises focused on local markets. There was no long-term planning, and the owners were the business. From 1850 to about 1900, more successful businesses started to develop administrative functions separate from their operations. Today we call them corporate staff. Two examples were John Jacob Astor's American Fur Company and Nicholas Biddle's Second Bank. But the Erie Railroad set the benchmark since its expansion required forward planning on a scale not yet seen in business.

Moving into the 1900s, the new century presented opportunities for vertical integration, as demonstrated by Gustavus Swift (meatpacking) and Singer sewing machines. Later in this phase, horizontal expansion was exhibited by the trusts and federations of the early 1900s. National Biscuit is cited as an example.

In the early twentieth century, these businesses had become moribund, so their structures evolved again. Multidivisional, decentralized structures were developed to make large, complex organizations more manageable. Moving to and through WWII, with the American economy growing to be the largest in the world, the old ways of doing things no longer worked. The four examples presented were DuPont (product focus), GM (divisional boundaries based on market strategy), Standard Oil (multi-departmental structure), and Sears (multidivisional organization).

This research was from the last century, before any form of modern technology existed. Are these theories still relevant? Yes. The globalization and supply chain issues of the last fifty years have forced businesses to reorganize yet again. Compartmentalized, just-in-time supply chains have replaced vertical integration. Look at how many logistics firms now exist. Look at the scale of FedEx, UPS, and DHL. Business systems have moved from timeshare to big iron, to desktops, to client/server, to the cloud. In each iteration, businesses have reorganized production planning, customer service, and administrative functions.

As businesses decide what functions they need to own versus outsource to be competitive, they have reorganized. Structure still follows strategy.

When you think about how you compete, is your business organized to deploy your strategy most effectively? If not, how should you reorganize your business?

Converting Theory Into Practice
For Your Business

While understanding Chandler and Porter is necessary to understand the big picture of competition, private company owners live in the "real world," so let's bring this down to what you live with every day.

You must get the strategy right first, but that is not enough. Then you must execute fearlessly and be ruthlessly loyal to the strategy. This chart sums up what I see in the market-place (see opposite page).

So how do you become a well-oiled machine? By thinking hard about your mission, vision, and key imperatives.

Mission is, "Who are we?"

Vision is, "Where are we going?"

Key imperatives show, "How are we going to get there?"

Figuring this out is what all companies need to do to be successful. But for most private companies, getting this right is difficult due to having fewer resources than larger, public companies.

(For a detailed example of how you can develop a winning strategy and drive execution for your company, see the BadgerCo Case Study in Appendix B.)

But having too much cash is also an issue.

Sustained Success Requires Both Strategy and Execution:

Strong	The Conversation Piece
	"All Talk, No Action"
	
	• Lots of meeting and
	  paralysis from analysis
	• History repeating itself
	• Finger pointing
		The Well-Oiled Machine
		"Focus & Alignment"
		
		• Great results and a
		  positive culture
		• Predictable outcomes
		• Empowered employees

Weak	The Hampster Wheel
	"Running in Place"
	
	• Reactive culture where
	  "firefighting" is the norm
	• Active politics
	• Decision by "no decision"
		The Ice Cream Shop
		"Flavor of the Day"
		
		• Bias for actions leads to
		  pattern of ready, fire, aim
		• Short-term focus
		• Chasing the next shiny
		  thing

Company Strategy (vertical axis)

Ability to Execute — Strong

(Graphic courtesy of Blue Oak Strategy, used with permission)

Building The Best Strategy To Drive Cash Allocation

For most businesses, cash allocation is a challenge. Margin pressure, seasonality, credit risk, and bank covenants make it a constant chore. Cash on hand is the oxygen of business. You can't run low and survive.

For successful businesses, the opposite is true. They have too much cash on hand. Apple is a well-discussed example. The public markets will force a resolution to Apple's cash hoard.

The Value Of Smart Cash Allocation

Here's an example: A client has built a successful business over two generations and has accumulated significant cash. The client does not need this cash on hand for operations. Being conservative, they have always saved for the future, and unless they find a major acquisition, this cash is not a productive asset for the family.

Frankly, they should find a better use for it or return the cash to shareholders.

These funds can be used to:

- Fund strategic growth initiatives
- Invest in diversifying strategies
- Pay down debt
- Increase compensation
- Provide peace of mind
- Support charitable causes

This family had achieved substantial success without having a formal strategic planning process. What worked well for them was remaining tightly focused on their niche and being excellent operators. That is why the cash accumulated over decades.

But as the competitive landscape changed, there were concerns that the future would not be as kind to them as the past. New regulations were causing concern. The next generation of leaders had different views than the founder. Some wanted to diversify revenue streams to reduce their risk, while others wanted to take more cash out of the business for personal use.

Furthermore, some were more aggressive than others in pursuing growth opportunities. Boards are stewards of the owners' capital. They should avoid under-utilizing assets and taking unwarranted risks, while sound business strategy and ownership priorities should drive cash allocation.

Creating A Strategy

The outside directors organized two parallel processes to help the family manage the issues. First, a traditional strategic planning process was started to help set priorities. Simply put, the family needed to set long-term priorities for the business. Fortunately, the family council was effective at this task.

Second, the board formed an investment committee to find top professional money managers who could manage a large sum of money. Personal chemistry was as much a part of the process as the mechanics of investing.

The board then connected the strategic priorities to the investment management program so that the investment policy (risk levels, distributions, volatility) supported those strategic priorities.

Good acquisition opportunities are few and far between in this industry. So, having ample cash on hand to be able to move quickly was important. This was included in developing the investment program—they could get cash to fund an acquisition, quickly if needed, with no strings attached.

The younger generation was in their forties, so they had a lot of time to worry about cash allocation. But this is where being too conservative may become a liability. Since lost opportunities compound as the market grows, not taking enough risk can become expensive over time.

Educating the family on market dynamics allowed decision-makers to define an investment strategy that:

- Supported the strategic priorities of the business
- Provided ample cash flow
- Allowed the older generation to sleep easy
- Excited the younger generation about future potential

The money managers also provided financial planning for the family members. Since each family executive now had a good idea of their situation, the transition between generations eased. The guesswork was removed, and the executives could focus on the business. This also took some stress out of family relations.

This example demonstrates how outside directors can help successful owners maximize opportunities and manage risk. Remember, too much cash is a good problem to have, but a problem nonetheless.

An ongoing challenge is to find the capital and talent to support your strategy. This dilemma is examined in the next chapter.

Your Ownership Journey

Secret #3. Business Strategy Drives Objectives, Then Tactics

» Strategy was once defined as trying to gain an unfair advantage in the marketplace.

» Strategy is done top-down; implementation is done bottom-up.

» If you have the right plan and execute the details properly, you should get the right results.

» Owners must master the five competitive forces; it only takes one to deprive you of success.

» Structure follows strategy; there is always a reason why industries and businesses are structured the way they are. Is your business structured for success?

» Since lost opportunities compound as the market grows, not taking enough risk can become very expensive over time.

Find Capital And Talent To Enable Strategy

Would you bet on Richard Baze or Laffit Pincay Jr.?

If you don't know, they are the two winningest horse race jockeys of all time. Their careers illustrate an important point about finding capital and talent.

Baze is the all-time win leader with 12,842 first-place finishes. Amazingly, he won about one out of four races he entered. Baze surpassed Pincay, who is second with 9,530 first-place finishes and won one out of five races.

However, Pincay is first in total earnings of $237,120,625, beating Baze by more than $36 million. Pincay won many more iconic races in his career, including the Kentucky Derby ('84), the Belmont Stakes ('82, '83, '84), and the Santa Anita Derby seven times.

During Baze's and Pincay's careers, bettors at the racetrack often cared more about these jockeys than the horses they rode. Something similar is true when it comes to finding capital and talent.

In racetrack parlance, when a capital source is writing a check, they are betting on the jockey, not the horse. The same is true when talent chooses to align with you.

That's because when thinking about raising capital, it all starts with the management team and its business plan. Likewise, when it comes to getting the right talent on board to enable your strategy, you are asking people to make a wager with their careers.

Capital Is Like Placing A Bet

Business is the confluence of people, money, ideas, and opportunities. You need to get all four, in the right proportions, to achieve commercial success. Money is a commodity. Whether it is debt or equity, how it is structured reflects how impactful the combination of people, ideas, and opportunities is.

Having spent years working in the venture capital and private equity arenas, I have heard, too often, people complain about how hard it is to raise capital for their business. But they have it backward.

Since General Georges Doriot started the venture capital industry in 1946, the truth has been that the market tends to fund worthy ideas and passes on the others. The capital markets are relatively efficient in that way, although they are certainly not perfect, either.[8]

When people complain, "If only I had the money," they are saying they are not presenting the market with something deserving the risk capital they are asking to be trusted with.

Raising Capital

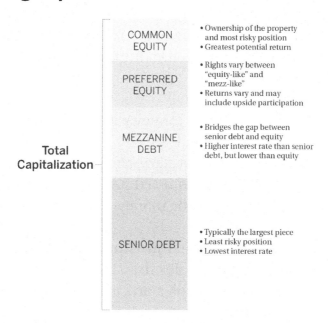

Funding sources need to know that you have a long-term competitive advantage in a well-defined market and that you deeply understand your customers' wants and needs, and how much they will pay for your products and services. Their desire to provide funding, and the terms thereof, reflect the value of what you are doing.

When you think about trading stocks and bonds, it isn't much different. On a financial exchange, everything is defined except for the price. The bids and asks are the price discovery process in action, with the final price being the definition of the fair value of that trade. This is the same as raising capital for your business but on a micro level.

The three steps to raising capital are: (1) set the business strategy and detailed planning, (2) decide how much and the form of capital to fund the plan, and (3) demonstrate that you can be trusted to return the money with a risk-adjusted amount of profit.

No one's going to give you money without details on your sources and uses of capital. So, you must be prepared to share your plan—a plan that allows the providers to get their money back with a risk-adjusted profit because without that, no one will give you the money.

You also must have a capital structure that lets you sleep at night. Because when sales drop 20 percent (e.g., due to COVID-19) and the bank starts calling, some owners don't have the stomach for it. If sales drop and your equity investors start calling, there's the old phrase: success has a thousand fathers, and failure is an orphan.[9]

Your capital structure includes all the capital used to support the business, including all debt and equity. Each structure has several variations—common stock, preferred equity, mezzanine debt, and senior debt. The goal is to have an efficient capital structure, which gives you the best return for the level of risk you're willing to accept.

As you move from top to bottom, the rewards decrease. Bondholders get their principal and interest, but nothing more. The common owners get the most upside since they have taken the most risk.

Successfully executing a business strategy requires capital and talent; let's examine both in detail.

Money Is A Raw Material

When you buy raw materials for your business, you usually look for the lowest cost for your specified need. You know what a pound of steel costs or how much it costs to ship a container from Shanghai to Los Angeles. Capital isn't much different; it is just another input. So, shouldn't you try to get the lowest cost of capital?

A firm's total cost of capital is a weighted average of the cost of equity and the cost of debt, known as the weighted average cost of capital (WACC).

Weighted Average Cost of Capital (WACC)

The formula for WACC looks complicated but is simple if you think it through:

WACC = (E/V x Re) + ((D/V x Rd) x (1 – T))

Where:

E = market value of the firm's equity (market cap)

V = total value of capital (equity plus debt)

E/V = percentage of capital that is equity

Re = cost of equity (required rate of return)

D = market value of the firm's debt

D/V = percentage of capital that is debt

Rd = cost of debt (yield to maturity on existing debt)

T = tax rate

To break it down further, you need to focus on:

- What rate of return do my equity investors require to reward the risk they are taking?
- If I am selling equity, how much of my business am I willing to give up?
- What interest rate does my bank demand to give me the loans I want?
- How much debt can the business handle so I can still sleep at night?

Owners need to weigh these trade-offs, such that they have the capital needed to fund their business plan and enough margin of safety so that if business gets soft, they comply with their debt covenants.

To re-emphasize, executing a business strategy requires both capital and talent. We examined capital structure issues, so now let's examine the need for talent to grow your business.

Sourcing Talent

Your ability to secure superior talent depends on many factors, but a competitive business strategy will tend to attract the best talent in a market. In most organizations, only a few people make the critical difference between success or failure. The rest are necessary to do the work, but they don't change the history of the enterprise. And that is okay; everyone needs a job. But as an owner, you need to understand which positions move the needle dramatically. An inspiring plan will attract people from afar to join you on your ownership journey.

Werner Wisdom

Observation: Almost all (95 percent) of people fill jobs where the job is defined first. The lucky people are the 5 percent who have jobs defined to suit them.

When you think about your leadership and management needs, consider where you want the business to be in three to five years. What will the organization chart look like then? What skills and experience will the leadership need to achieve those goals?

This is another case of starting with the answer and working backward to today to build a plan to get you there.

Do you have those people today? Can you develop your current staff to get there? If so, how will you do it? Are there gaps that will force you to hire from the outside? If so, how long will that take, and how do you make sure they are cultural fits?

To use a baseball metaphor, it's like having a rebuilding season, where you want a few new players but must work within the salary cap. You need some talent, so you're going to make some trades. You also move some of your current players around so that the team on the field has the best chance of winning within your financial constraints.

So, let's look at how to evaluate talent and fit, since you will need to do that whether you are considering internal promotions or hiring from the outside.

Personality, style, and cultural fit usually determine whether someone can be successful or not. While this may be as much an art as a science, there is science to rely on.

Many tools can be used to bring some intelligence to the process. Here are a few examples:

- Predictive Index
- Riso-Hudson Enneagram Type Indicator
- Myers-Briggs Test
- Jung Personality Test
- DISC
- Holland Code

While these are scientific and need an expert to conduct and properly interpret, the Skill/Will model is a bit more practical, although it has its limitations. The Skill/Will Matrix was derived from the situational leadership model created by Paul Hersey and Ken Blanchard in the 1970s. Blanchard was one of the authors of the book, *The One Minute Manager*.

For internal candidates up for promotion, the issue is likely to be how to develop them so they have the necessary skills and experience to do the job. We say experience when we mean judgment. At senior levels, judgment is what matters since it drives decisions and behaviors down the line.

Development is a process, not a decision. Like most processes, it needs to be managed, and that means it needs a plan. Development plans usually start by identifying career goals and the employee's actions needed to meet these goals. These plans should be written, time certain, and reviewed regularly. Here is a simplified example of a development plan of a junior social media employee:

Development Plans

Invest in Your People By Developing Them		
• Encourage growth and development by identifying career goals and actions the employee can take to meet these goals. • Usually given to everyone within an organization.		
Action Step Target	**Complete Date Goal**	**Complete Date**
1. 2Q — Spend one hour per week researching current content trends	7/1/2022	
2. Attend national social media seminar in August	9/1/2022	
3. Onboard three new client accounts, successfully manage them for at least one quarter	7/1/2022	
4. Allocate 5 hours per month with industry leader/mentor	9/1/2022	
5. Achieve next level technical certification	12/31/2022	

Do A Gap Analysis

What is a gap analysis? It is the thinking required to clearly state the difference between the talent you need in the future and what you have today. Do you need a senior digital marketing leader? Do you need a supply chain guru? Is anyone doing this for you today?

You find the gap by comparing today's organization chart to the future organization chart you just designed. Then, for each box on the chart, list the skills, experience, relationships, and personalities that describe the perfect candidate. This is often an iterative process for each position since you are building a team, and how the team works together is what matters.

For older organizations that need to inject new skills (e.g., digital), the leading candidates will likely be earlier in their careers. They may be the functional or technical leader, but they may lack the experience and wisdom of years needed for people to follow them. Balancing those types of trade-offs is the critical part of building a cohesive team.

The second part of the gap analysis is timing. You may have good people in development, but will they be ready to step up to the challenge when you need them? If they need another three to five years to mature, that may be too late. Having a detailed development plan for top staff will help you answer this question.

The four parts of a development plan are:

- Identifying teachable skills and scheduling that schooling (e.g., accounting, finance, marketing)
- Making sure the candidate gets critical experiences to help them develop judgment
- Providing direction on behaviors to reinforce and those that need to be modified
- Creating opportunities for the candidate to deliver results through other employees, which is harder than being a strong individual contributor

---

Werner Wisdom

When hiring at the executive level, the hiring decision is often, "What can you live without?" versus "What must you have?"

The last part of the gap analysis is what I like to call the daisy chain effect. When you pull up one person to a higher level, what happens to the void created? Is there someone ready to step in or not? Nature abhors a vacuum, and so do organizations. Your development plans need to run from top to bottom. It keeps going down until you find an excess supply of talent qualified to fill the lower positions.

In summary, you need to identify the key decisions, track the transition milestones, and manage the underlying details to pull it all together. A traditional Gantt chart will work, but there are a variety of other tools for this purpose.

Key Succession Decisions

Think Through the Consequences of Each Decision		
Decision To Make	New Positions	Vacated Positions
Position to fill		
Key deliverables (12/24/26 mo)		
Leading internal candidates?		
Development needs?		
External recruiting plan (if needed)		
Compensation range		
Who needs to know to help make this candidate successful?		
Who is negatively impacted?		
Open issues to consider?		

Establish Transition Milestones

			Manage The Details Carefully				
Position	Internal/ External	Fully Effective Date	Development Leadtime	Start Dev Date	Recruit Leadtime	Kickoff Date
VP Sales	Internal (A)	Jan 2023	12 mo	Jan 2022	N/A	Oct 2021
Regional Sales	External	June 2023	N/A	N/A	3 mo	Mar 2023
CFO	External	Jan 2022	N/A	N/A	6 mo	July 2021
VP Service	Internal (B)	Dec 2022	6 mo	July 2022	3 mo (C)	July 2022

(A) — Two candidates identified and mostly qualified
(B) — Three candidates, all need development, 50% likely need to go outside
(C) — Make decision Sept 2022 if need to go outside to fill

Track The Details

		Who Do You Tell What & When?				
Position Title	Incumbent Name	Retirement Date	Number of Candidates	Candidate(s) Name(s)	Readiness Ratings
CEO	Mark Graves	12/2026	2	Alice Walker, Jack Brown	8.0 6.5
Director of Sales	Janet Sanders	02/2022	1	Riley Notts	9.0
Head of Human Resources	Matthew Snipe	12/2023	3	Margaret Jones, Eliot Park, Elizabeth Maxey	9.5 8.5 8.0

Communication Plan

Who Do You Tell What & When?

➤ What do participants need to know to make career decisions?

➤ What influences the retention of others?

➤ What is confidential?

➤ What do you want to broadcast internally and externally?

The last part of the program, and perhaps the most important, is communication. Since we are talking about humans, communication is almost always the issue that drives success or failure. Several constituencies want and need to know the talent plans: the winning candidates, the losing candidates, the future followers, customers, suppliers, and investors.

Each constituency has a different need, so the message and the timing of the message will be different. You want to control the message and the timing since there is so much risk and uncertainty in the outcome.

To create your communications plan, think about these questions:

- What do constituents need to know to do their job?
- What do candidates need to know to make their career decisions?
- What may influence the retention of other employees?
- What information is confidential?
- What is beneficial or harmful to broadcast internally and externally?
- How can you maintain flexibility in the process?

Attracting, training, and retaining executive talent is one of the toughest issues for a private company. But when recruiting board members, consider other complexities.

Soliciting Initial Outside Directors For Private Companies

Private and family-owned companies with tenured outside directors have learned how to attract, evaluate, and retain other outsider directors. Experienced directors create value by leveraging their knowledge and well-established relationships to effect change. But where does this start? A critical step to recruiting initial directors is to understand that candidates likely lack institutional knowledge and have no meaningful relationships with current directors or the company.

Private companies seeking their initial outside directors are typically mature businesses in their second or third generation of leadership. They have experienced multiple business cycles, and the leadership is self-aware. They are looking for outsiders to fill specific needs.

Then there are the smart entrepreneurs who don't wait to ask for help. They understand their limitations and seek outside counsel early in the company's development. This is more common with technology-related companies. Due to their high growth rate, they need advice sooner.

In both cases, they often engage consultants to lead them through this process.

Werner Wisdom

You are only a leader if you can get people to follow you.
Otherwise, you are walking alone.

The consultants help the owners design the new board (how many directors, insiders/outsiders, candidate criteria, compensation, nominating process) and manage the selection process. The first request for resumes is typically described in a one-page anonymous summary. Once an initial phone interview is scheduled, candidates receive a two- to three-page description of the business. Sometimes they receive a marketing/sales presentation from a recent sales meeting. While useful, these documents lack context.

While this practice is sufficient to run the process, it is also one-sided. The consultants are properly focused on the needs of the owners, not the needs of the candidates. The candidates may experience a series of surprises as the discussion unfolds. How does that help to expedite the best matches? While a partner in a private equity fund, we would receive hundreds of investment summaries each year before signing non-disclosure agreements. These teasers were usually two pages long and told our firm what we needed to determine if we should commit resources to a project. The company summaries I have seen as a board candidate have a fraction of the typical investment summary content.

Candidates are deciding if they should invest a significant amount of personal time and accept reputational risk when they evaluate joining a new board. My experience suggests that the selection process would be improved if it was less opaque.

Key Questions To Consider
The critical point to consider is that outside candidates

for director seats frequently have little or no institutional knowledge, no sense of the company's culture, and little or no critical business data when they submit their resumes to the search committee. While the current board, owners, and consultants are intrinsically in tune with these issues, the candidates are not. They are often recruited from different industries. Professionals seeking board seats will "opt-in" until they have a reason to leave the process. Better information will accelerate the weaning process.

After reviewing a dozen searches that I have been involved in, I have concluded that these four questions need to be considered when designing the search:

- *What non-public data do we provide to the candidates, and when do we provide it?*

This is the most difficult of the four questions since there may not be much precedent to provide guidance. Other than its bank, the company likely has not shared critical information with any outsider. The best first step is to consider, "What would I want to know if it were me?" but remember that the incentives are not the same.

- *How do we build and test relationships through the process?*

Phone interviews are an effective first screen, but good relationships grow through mutually shared experiences. A good process usually includes an opening dinner, with a full day of meetings the next day, including site tours. These tours should highlight major product lines and capabilities and a chance to socialize with the full management team. The more time spent together, the better.

- *If the company is looking for multiple initial outside directors, what can it do to test the compatibility between candidates?*

Since the outside seats are typically slotted for specific skills, consider scheduling non-competing candidates (e.g., a finance person and a marketing person) together for onsite interviews to create interactions you can observe. I participated in this once and found it beneficial. Meeting other candidates allows them to gauge the talent pool and understand where the process is headed. I have been on boards where the initial outsiders learn of each other when they shake hands at the first meeting. That approach extends the time needed to build effective relationships.

- *How do we structure the recruitment process to dovetail into the onboarding process?*

Plan the onboarding process first and work backward. Part of this depends on the committee structure and the interviewing with committee needs (e.g., audit, compensation, nominating). Matching people for committee discussions, separate from the full board, will expedite onboarding.

It is important to remember why outsiders serve on private boards. The reasons to serve as an outside director for a private company are (1) to have a meaningful impact on the organization, (2) to expand their network, (3) for professional growth, and (4) to stay engaged for those who are at or near retirement. While the compensation provides respect for the time spent at meetings, it is usually not the prime motivation. Successful professionals serve as outside directors because they want to. Over a typical three-year term, there will be enough late flights, early wakeups, difficult conversations, and calendar conflicts to de-motivate the candidates incented only by money. Better data will allow outsiders to understand their impact, and stronger relationships will motivate them to act.

Soliciting Candidates

The typical board meets quarterly, with a few calls between meetings. Many private boards do not have formal audit, compensation, and governance subcommittees. This reduces the opportunities to work together. I have found that in these situations, newcomers may need a full year to become integrated.

When soliciting candidates for initial outsider director positions, consider providing more than a few descriptive pages to brief the candidates. Most, if not all, of this will be revealed no later than their first board meeting. In addition to improving the interview process, you will likely receive fresh ideas to improve your business.

Data To Help The Candidate Understand The Business

- Strategic Plan
- Three-year audited financial statements
- Pro-forma forward budget
- Summary of credit facilities
- Organization chart
- Status of Management succession plans
- Executive appraisal/incentive systems
- Union/labor history

Once directors know each other, they will naturally start talking offline, which is the best way to build good working relationships. The goal is to have a strong, collegial environment that welcomes constructive dissent, fosters resolution, and promotes good governance. While cost is always a concern, consider inviting candidates to a few more meetings, plant tours, or sales events early in their terms. Since the expected term is measured in years, amortizing these travel costs over twenty-four to thirty-six months may make it an easy decision.

As the process moves forward, the best candidates will understand the risk of being a director. As a fiduciary, they will both want and need this information.

Data To Help The Candidate Evaluate D&O Risk

- History of communications to outside and family shareholders
- By-laws with indemnifications
- Domicile-specific director obligations
- Minutes of past board meetings
- Insurance summary — all lines
- Summary of claims, settlements, judgments
- Dividend policy
- Audit committee reports
- Compliance manual
- HR policy manual
- Special directives from owners
- List of professionals: attorneys, bankers, accountants, auditors, consultants

---

Electing outside directors is a commitment measured in years. Many companies purposely limit the information they provide to candidates, either from habit or due to competitive fear. The habit will need to disappear when the outsiders are elected, and the fear is often not justified. Providing timely, critical datasets and multiple opportunities to build personal relationships are critical to selecting and onboarding the best outside directors. It is a learning process for the owners, frequently more so than for the candidates.

Werner Wisdom

As the saying goes: "You don't really understand something until you can teach it to someone else."

Agents Of Change: The Advantages Of Non-Executive Directors

Whether a company is public or private, the mission of its board of directors is to provide leadership in key issues: oversight, strategy, capital structure, succession planning, and risk management. While regulators will enforce matters at public companies, non-executive directors are often the only external force to drive change at private companies.

So long as the bank is happy and the taxes are paid, private and family business owners can drift off course for a while. Effective outside directors may need to be the "adult in the room" to keep the business healthy and the insiders focused on the business' best interests.

Effective Non-Executive Directors Start With Accountability

Aside from providing broader business experience and corporate governance duties, company and advisor firms cite "checks and balances" as one of the main advantages of non-executive directors, according to the QCA 2020 Non-Executive Director Survey.[10]

Holding management accountable is one of a board's highest obligations and one of the greatest advantages of non-executive directors. Here are three examples that will test the leadership within a business. In each scenario, you can see trouble ahead:

- A family executive lacks the talent and passion needed to run the business.
- A tenured, loyal employee has risen to a senior position well above his or her competency.
- The industry has been disrupted by technology or foreign competition, and the company is unable to respond.

The solutions don't come from spreadsheets or a new app. They come from determined individuals standing up to work through the issue. In these examples, the outsiders need to be the change agents.

Characteristics Of Effective Independent Directors

If you are a non-executive director at a private company, most likely, you are there to make sure these situations get dealt with constructively.

To be successful at these matters, outside directors who bring positive results need to hold three convictions:

1. Bad news does not get better with time.
2. Work the business issue and avoid the personality flaws.
3. You were elected to lead on the tough issues. Now is the time to perform.

In a recent situation, our board was dealing with a long-standing CEO who did not have the skills and personality to lead the business through a season of disruptive change. While a valued employee and close friend of the non-executive owner, this was the wrong person to take the business forward. Separating the CEO meant rupturing a fifteen-year friendship.

As the lead outside director, I was responsible for driving the process through evaluation, decision-making, separation, and the eventual transition process. The trick was getting the owner to put aside his personal loyalties and focus on the business needs.

After a tense board meeting, the decision was finally made to separate the CEO; there was no other option given the details of the situation. The CEO needed to hear this from the owner to know that there was no room for negotiation. The owner was a technologist, not a businessperson. After much introspection, the owner realized he didn't know how to get through this without letting his emotions interfere.

External Directors Recognize
When Third-Party Counsel Is Needed

When the owner asked me, "How should I handle this?" I realized that to fulfill my duty as the lead external director, I needed to step into the situation even deeper. With counsel, we prepared the owner for each of the likely scenarios that might arise during the termination process. I told the owner to expect to feel uncomfortable; this is not supposed to be easy. Be respectful, direct, and stay focused on the business issues, not the personalities.

The CEO's mismanagement also meant there was little cash available to fund a severance package. A reasonable offer was made, but the CEO pushed back, threatening multiple lawsuits for discrimination and nuisance claims. After turning down the rhetoric and asking a few pointed questions, we understood what was important to him. So, we traded away a few restrictive covenants to avoid giving away cash and quickly achieved closure.

Outside directors are often the only force that can break a stalemate or provide leadership to take a private company through a perilous situation. This is one of the key reasons private companies should seek competent and effective non-executive directors to provide strong leadership when they need it most.

What comes next? With the talent and capital in place, it is time to execute your growth strategy. That is the focus of the following chapter.

Your Ownership Journey

Secret #4. Ownership Strategy Comes First

» Money is a commodity. Whether it is debt or equity, how it is structured reflects the impact of the combination of people, ideas, and opportunities.

» The three steps to raising capital are: (1) set the business strategy and support it with detailed planning, (2) decide how much and the form of capital to fund the plan, and (3) demonstrate that you can be trusted to return the money with a risk-adjusted amount of profit.

» Even if you find the perfect deal, you still need to be sure that you are compatible with your new partners.

» In most organizations, only a few people make the critical difference between success or failure.

» When you think about your leadership and management needs, consider where you want the business to be in three to five years. What will the organization chart look like then?

» Effective outside directors are often the "adult in the room" to keep the business healthy and the insiders focused on the business' best interests.

» Outside directors are sometimes the only force that can break a stalemate or provide the leadership to take a private company through a perilous situation.

Execute Organic Growth And M&A To Achieve The Strategy

Most CEOs have bold growth plans. Do you?

In a 2021 Fortune/Deloitte CEO Survey, 110 leading CEOs representing more than fifteen industries shared a perspective on the new shape of a CEO agenda that may lead organizations out of the pandemic.[11]

According to the survey results summary:

> *While CEOs may be divided on the duration of pandemic business effects more generally, their bullish outlook on the future of their own organizations is remarkably in sync. Seventy-seven percent of CEOs say they expect their organization's growth to be strong over the next 12 months. About a third say "very strong," about half say "strong," and about a quarter expect only "modest" growth. Notably, no CEOs are expecting anything less ("weak" or "very weak").*

"CEOs are optimistic about the year ahead, expecting strong growth fueled by innovation and pent-up consumer demand," says Joe Ucuzoglu, CEO of Deloitte US.

How To Execute A Growth Strategy

What are your expectations of growth to achieve your strategies?

Consider this as a process. You will hear this many times in this book since it is one of the best pieces of advice I was given. Start by determining what level of organic growth and/or mergers or acquisitions is needed to achieve the business strategy. Having that foundational information is important, but good ideas and planning aren't worth much if the execution is lacking.

How much of your future growth will be organic, and what is needed to make it happen? If organic growth does not achieve your goals, then acquisitions need to be considered. If you need to make acquisitions, what are the targets, and how will you successfully acquire and integrate them?

When we say organic growth, we mean growing your business as you have done in the past: winning new customers, adding new product lines, and adding new distribution channels. This is what you know how to do.

But you can take a more sophisticated approach. While your entrepreneurial instincts will drive your actions, take a moment to think, "Is there another way to achieve better results?"

- Is your competitive advantage as sharp as you think it is? If not, what should you do to sharpen it?
- How strong is your brand? What can you do to enhance it?

- What other products or services can you sell to your current customers?
- From what other distribution channels do your customers buy your product?
- Is your digital strategy effective? For older businesses, do you even have a digital strategy?

These are just a handful of questions to consider when you are trying to increase your growth rate. While some of these issues may require capital, it is more about getting the right talent to make things happen.

Previously we spoke about "working in the business" versus "working on the business." This is where those two concepts connect. You need to be both strategic and tactical to get the best result. The strategic analysis requires a full understanding of the business, the capabilities of the team, the balance sheet, the industry dynamics, and a strong gut check on practical constraints that never show up in a spreadsheet.

Chandler's message of "structure follows strategy" and Porter's model of competition are what you need to understand to develop an effective growth strategy.

An effective growth strategy and the practical tactics to implement it are essential to driving organic growth. But having the discipline to stay the course is equally if not more important. Many owners get comfortable and lose their drive once they have some success. This is one of several reasons why businesses stagnate. Having the drive and discipline to keep pushing forward is what distinguishes the best businesses.

About Acquisitions

Chandler and Porter are also the starting point to think about acquisitions. Some people are deal junkies and must be buying something to press their joy button. That is the wrong reason to make an acquisition. The real questions to consider are:

- How does it increase the value of my business?
- How does it increase my competitive advantage?
- What does it do (to quote Warren Buffett) to "widen the moat around my castle"?

This process should help you to identify specific criteria for what to buy. How big is big enough to move your needle but not so big that you choke on it? How do their products complement your existing product line? Are you trying to take out a competitor or acquire critical talent by buying their business? You need specific criteria and analysis so that as you move through the acquisition process, you have a North Star to guide you.

Werner Wisdom

Sometimes the best deal is the one you don't do.

Once you have sound logic for what to do, go to market to identify targets that meet your criteria.

As the targets come into focus and the field narrows, start to ask yourself, "How am I going to pay for this, and what is my internal rate of return?" This is a good time to return to Secret #4 to refresh yourself on capital structure, WACC, and the efficient use of capital. Worthy deals will get financed because they make economic sense. Putting together the right economics is what the sponsor (you) must do to be trusted with other people's money.

If you have never done a deal before, what do you need to know to raise capital for your first acquisition? Here are ten steps to help you understand the process.

1. What Is Being Acquired?

   You need to start by defining what is being acquired and why it makes sense to the capital sources. This is why we have reviewed competitive advantage, industry dynamics, and talent. Your capital sources will review these in your first conversation and will likely return to them throughout the discussion. If they don't believe in your investment thesis, they will walk away. Revenue, EBITDA, growth rates, debt levels, industry growth rate, competitive factors, and management talent will be discussed in the first thirty minutes.

2. Why Does The Deal Make Sense To The Buyer?

   The first step is to set the stage for why the deal makes sense. If you are reaching out to financial buyers for assistance, then you need to understand that financial buyers (private equity funds) are economic creatures who will want to talk through from entry (when they buy it) to exit (when they sell it). Equity analysts use this same process for public company stocks.

Strategic buyers are different. They are going to buy the business once and intend to own it indefinitely. The assumption is that they will fully integrate it into their larger enterprise. Typically, the acquired business fades away over time unless the brand has value of its own. If you own the business, you are the strategic buyer.

3. Financial Projections

Once you have set the stage, it is time to see if the numbers make sense. You need to develop a financial model that shows the P&L, balance sheet, and cash flows over three to five years. This model is based on assumptions, and the assumptions need to be clearly stated so that the capital source can judge your aggressiveness and if they are comfortable with that level of risk.

The punchline on the model is not, "How much money do we make?" Rather, capital sources will focus on the margin of safety of your debt service and the internal rate of return (IRR) on the new equity used to fund the deal. Banks only loan money when they are confident it will be returned, with interest, when they want it back. Equity sources provide risk capital when they believe the returns are enough to justify the risk of losing it all.

4. Stock Versus Asset Deals

The form of the transaction is the next question. Is it a stock deal or an asset deal? In a stock deal, the buyer assumes all the liabilities that may come from whatever happened in the past (e.g., employee lawsuits from years before or product liability claims from prior sales). In an asset deal, the buyer picks what they want, and the seller keeps the rest.

Obviously, sellers prefer a stock deal, and buyers prefer asset deals. Asset deals are more common with small businesses and become impractical as businesses grow. They are common in bankruptcy and turnaround situations, where the seller is trying to wash away debts they can't pay.

Asset deals can be clean. Stock deals become more complicated. In an asset deal, the buyer can value individual assets, and that becomes the price. A stock deal has more intangibles to value, so more risk to the buyer. That is why earn-outs are common; they are a way to share the risk and keep the seller focused on ensuring the buyer gets what was agreed upon.

5. Net Working Capital At Close

Stock deals ordinarily assume at the closing the

business is cash-free and debt-free. That means the seller keeps all the cash but also must pay off any debts. But the buyer needs assurance that there is enough working capital to run the business. The buyer doesn't want to write a second check to make the first payroll after the deal closes.

This is known as the net working capital requirements of the deal and is a key part of negotiations. This is the final calculation that determines how much cash the seller gets at closing.

6. Escrow, Baskets, And Caps

As the lawyers get to work, there will be discussion around escrow, baskets, and caps. These are legal mechanisms to apportion risk between the parties. Things can and do go wrong after the deal, and buyers want a mechanism to make sellers pay for issues that are their responsibility.

In each contract, there will be representations (often called "reps") and warranties from both parties, as well as indemnifications. On the sell side, there will be two sets—one set made by the company and a second set made by individual owners. If there is a default on ownership issues after the deal, there is no business paying for the legal defense. This should be a concern for the seller. Since these are usually considered "fundamental representations," if something goes wrong, it will be a problem.

These issues are so serious that buyers will likely require funds to be placed in escrow to make sure there is cash to pay the damages.

For example, the agreement may be that 5 percent of the value is held in escrow for one year to pay for specified issues. The triggers to break escrow need to be specific. If nothing goes wrong, after the year, the buyer gets what is left in escrow.

Sometimes it makes sense to remember that the small stuff isn't worth arguing about. So the buyer will agree to accept the first $100,000 of problems, but above that, the seller pays from the escrow. This reduces disputes when the parties still need to work together.

As a result of these market forces, insurance companies have developed reps and warranty (R&W) insurance to cover some of these claims. Each policy is specific to a deal. Buyers like R&W insurance since it makes it easier to price a deal and know there are funds to pay the claims. Sellers like R&W insurance since it helps them sleep at night.

7. Capital Structure Design

Once you figure out what the business is worth and how to structure the deal, you need to decide how to structure the capital stack to attract the right amounts and forms of capital. This was covered in Secret #4.

8. Deal Costs

Doing deals is not cheap. For the buyers, they need to pay for lawyers, accountants, and consultants. Sellers may need to pay for investment bankers, accountants, consultants, and capital gains taxes.

The need for consultants depends on the industry and how sophisticated the buyers and sellers may be. Owners who have never done a deal before should be wary when they sell their business. It is the most important decision of their career, and they may have little or no preparation for it. There is more art than science to picking an investment banker and legal team, managing quality of earnings (QoE) and diligence, and completing a transaction.

Werner Wisdom

No matter how big and sophisticated your deal team is, you walk the last mile alone. There is only a deal when the buyer and seller meet eye to eye and hammer out the last few sensitive issues that the professionals cannot negotiate on your behalf.

A QoE report is when financial experts take a deep dive into your revenue, profits, balance sheet, and cash flows and normalize them to how a buyer would view the business. This is like a Good Housekeeping Seal of Approval that your books and records comply with GAAP (generally accepted accounting principles). It calls out what you do different and adjusts your private company expenses (eg, the owner's kids are on the payroll even when they are still in grade school).

Sellers sometimes pay for a QoE early in the process since it is easier to sell the deal. It also gives them time to fix problems before buyers find them and reduce the price accordingly. Buyers like to pay for QoE to make sure it is their trusted advisor doing the work. More commonly, sellers pay for a QoE, and then buyers have their source double-check the QoE to know it is trustworthy.

9. Sources And Uses

In addition to "net working capital," the phrase "sources and uses" needs to be understood. Practically, it states where all the funds are coming from to execute the deal and where they are going. For sources, it will include new debt, equity, and rollover capital from the seller. The uses side shows what stays in the business, what goes to the sellers, and anything else involved in the deal. A more detailed approach shows the allocation of capital to various growth initiatives.

For example, in a $100 million transaction, it might be that $60 million goes to the sellers, and $40 million is used to grow the business. Of that, $20 million is equity for new acquisitions (bolt-ons), and $20 million is to fund organic growth.

This statement sums up the deal and forces the parties to make sure everything ties out. Until you have a draft of sources and uses, you may not know how it will work.

The sellers need this to calculate net proceeds. From the gross proceeds, they need to deduct expenses for the bankers, lawyers, accountants, consultants, and capital gains taxes. A useful rule of thumb is that net proceeds will be about two-thirds of gross proceeds, based on the current federal capital gains rates of 20 percent.

10. Deal Execution

While all the above is true, the most important thing to remember is that it "ain't over until it's over" or "the eagle has landed." Pick your cliché, but they are often used for good reason.

I have experienced several transactions where, even after six to nine months of hard work, the deal falls apart at the closing table for some reason. Buyers can "flake out" for any reason or no reason at all. Sellers decide at the last minute that they can't part with the family legacy. It all happens.

For these reasons, the strategy and planning provided at the beginning of this section are intended to provide you with a path to success. If the strategy and planning are good and the deal makes sense, it will likely get done. If buyers or sellers don't spend the time up-front to be thoughtful, it is more likely that time and money will be wasted on a deal that falls apart along the way.

That Company May Be Good To Own, But Tough To Buy

At a client's recent board meeting, we evaluated making a bid on a rival business worth $100 million. It was a "bet the farm" decision. Our management had spent years positioning itself for the opportunity to obtain this business, and now that acquisition was finally upon us. Even though it was an extremely large transaction for the buyer, the bank was prepared to provide financing, thanks to a strong relationship. The transaction would catapult this second-generation business into a higher league. The younger generation was itching for growth. It would be a defining moment for the business.

The natural growth rate of the industry is slightly less than the gross domestic product (GDP). The industry was filled with cash cows but few shooting stars. It is heavily regulated, and the regulations vary by state, so this was the only attractive target adjacent to the core market, allowing for economies of scale by combining operations.

Our due diligence process revealed material differences in how we ran the same type of business. Labor utilization, management depth, and compensation methods were all contrasting. Their differences made for a much more profitable business. But we also knew that the seller had a reputation for being a substandard place to work, and it was unclear what employment law risks they were taking to obtain better financial performance.

A successful acquisition and integration would produce a dominant market force and significant cash flows for the owners. There would not be another opportunity like this in the buyer's core market, likely in their lifetime.

Everyone was enthusiastic about the opportunity until I raised the unexpected question: "What is the IRR, and how are we going to pay for it?" The excitement of the opportunity, coupled with the fact that we could fund the acquisition, caused people to forget that basic but important question: How would we get our money back, plus a profit, for taking the risk, and how much profit was required to justify the risk? After all, an acquisition of this size effectively bets the company on a single decision with no way to back out.

This was about buying cash flows and customers, since it would not take the buyer into new products, new markets, or complementary industries. The target was already lean, so there were limited cost-reduction opportunities. The growth rates were nominal, so we could not rely on growth to generate IRR. Financial engineering would help, but the buyer did not want too much leverage since they had experienced severe downturns in the industry in the past. How else do you pay for an acquisition?

The math didn't work. Even though it would be a great business to own, and the financing was available, the deal was underwater. It was a classic case of being a good business to own but a tough business to buy. Acquisitions can be exciting, but that doesn't mean they should be executed. Sometimes choosing not to act is the right decision, though inaction may feel less satisfying.

Weighing Your Options

Even if your company has spent years weighing its options as to whether or not to acquire what your managers believe (and hope) to be a lucrative deal, there may still be questions to answer before purchasing. The bigger the deal's price tag, scale, and complexity, the greater need for careful reflection. There may be contrasting methods where the management, compensation, and/or labor are concerned, and these contrasts are not to be taken lightly. Before signing on the dotted line, raise the questions:

- What is the IRR?
- How do we pay for it?
- How will we get our money back, plus risk?
- Is the risk too great?
- How much profit is necessary to justify the risk?
- Finally, the most important question: Should we do it?

If the higher-ups in your company agree that the acquisition is worth the risk, and everyone can come to the same conclusions when all the data is in, congratulations, you have yourself a brand-new company. If not, you will most likely be glad you asked the questions you did, subsequently saving yourself a lot of money, time, and heartache. The dissatisfaction of choosing not to do a deal is a far better outcome than buyer's remorse.

Sleep Better With Reps
And Warranties Insurance

When boards are deliberating the purchase or sale of a business, they need to consider the long-term risks of the decision. Understanding the representations, warranties, and indemnifications being made is essential to executing fiduciary duty since the risks do not go away after the deal is done.

Managing risk is one of the primary responsibilities of the board. The board has three choices: risks can be ignored, managed, or insured by a third party at a cost. As part of considering a transaction, boards need to determine if reps and warranties (R&W) insurance is needed and/or required as part of the deal.

To begin, business owners need to know the difference between representations, warranties, and indemnities. Representations are factual statements about the state of the company meant for drawing in the buyer; warranties are assurances that the representations are true. Indemnities are a promise to reimburse the other party if the reps and warranties are breached.

My experience over the years is that sellers get excited about a price but fail to fully understand the representations, warranties, and indemnifications they provide in exchange for the cash. Over time, people tend to forget about how great the price was but live with regret for obligations they endure that money can't make it go away. Getting sellers to truly understand reps, warranties, and indemnities is essential to a good deal.

The opposite of risk is opportunity, and the ability to ensure the representations and warranties may give one party a competitive advantage in negotiations.

After completing a thorough diligence process, buyers usually have one or two issues that are difficult to get comfortable with; sellers usually know when they have exposure that they can't manage.

Owners often accept risks they know and understand or risks that they know they cannot change. Buyers don't want to take any risks they don't have to and don't take any risks they can push back on the seller.

This is why insurance companies sell R&W insurance. It allows buyers and sellers to sell certain risks to a third party with defined limits and exposures. While most people don't like paying for insurance, it may be the only way to bridge a gap in negotiations. R&W insurance has been available in the US since the 1990s.

Components Of R&W Insurance

R&W insurance and D&O (directors and officers liability insurance) policies serve different purposes. D&O protects officers, directors, and the company. R&W insurance serves the shareholders of the company. This is because shareholders make certain reps, warranties, and indemnifications individually, not the company.

Policies have four major components:

- **Escrow:** The amount of money that the buyer requires the seller to set aside to compensate the buyer for breaches of reps and warranties.
- **Cap:** The upper limit of damages that a buyer will pursue the seller for recovery.
- **Basket/Threshold:** This amount serves as the deductible of the policy.
- **Survival Period:** The number of years the reps and warranties are enforceable.

R&W insurance is usually available for deals between $25 million and $1 billion enterprise value.

Sellers buy R&W insurance to sleep easier at night. With insurance, they can move forward with their lives, investing the proceeds without worrying about a clawback.

Buyers seek R&W insurance so that in case of a breach, they do not need to chase individual owners who have likely dispersed, may be unsophisticated, or have spent their proceeds and be unable to pay what they owe to the buyer.

Smart buyers use R&W insurance to gain an advantage in negotiations. With R&W insurance, they can set smaller escrow amounts, lower caps, and shorter survival periods, thereby appearing more attractive to the seller. Buyers purchase R&W insurance for these reasons.

The Cost Of R&W Insurance

Like all insurance, the client must go through an under-writing process. For R&W insurance, there are two steps: indication and quotation. Initial, non-binding indications can be provided in a week or two. To receive a binding quotation, clients must pay a non-refundable underwriting fee (usually $10,000 to $30,000) to the underwriter. Firm quotes are typically available in a week or two.

Premiums for R&W insurance usually run at 2 percent to 4 percent of the coverage, with a minimum retention (deductible) of 1.5 percent. The policy period should match the reps and warranties. Beyond that, the terms of the policy are negotiable since it is a contract between parties.

At smaller private companies, R&W insurance is typically too expensive, and therefore not a good option. Attorneys for these firms will usually advise clients to negotiate an out-of-court settlement and avoid litigation if there is a claim against them.

At larger private companies where the costs are manageable, R&W insurance becomes more appealing since litigation is more common. It is easy to think about R&W insurance as paying a fixed amount now to avoid possibly paying a large, unknown amount later.

At a private company with a fiduciary board, the directors must decide if R&W insurance is needed and provide the required coverage. At a private company without a board, R&W insurance is about letting the owners sleep better at night. For the buyers, this is about managing buyers' risks and avoiding hassles post-close if things go south.

What comes next is proper governance. That will be explored in-depth in the following chapter.

Your Ownership Journey

Secret #5. Execute Organic Growth And M&A To Achieve The Strategy

» A great growth strategy is useless if the leadership does not have the discipline to stay focused and execute the plan. It is important to avoid shiny object syndrome on your way to success.

» There is a market for buying and selling companies, just like any other market. If you don't understand the market, take some time to get educated before betting your business.

» Reward is about numbers; risk is about judgment.

» Acquisitions can be exciting, but that doesn't mean they should be executed. Sometimes choosing not to act is the right decision, though inaction may feel less satisfying in the moment.

» The bigger the deal's price tag, scale, and complexity, the greater need for an outside perspective.

SECRET #6

Assess And Develop Proper Governance

Albert Einstein could have been talking about business governance when he said, "If people are good only because they fear punishment and hope for reward, then we are a sorry lot indeed."

Perhaps Mark Goyder, founder of a business-led think tank, said it best: "Governance and leadership are the yin and the yang of successful organizations. If you have leadership without governance, you risk tyranny, fraud, and personal fiefdoms. If you have governance without leadership, you risk atrophy, bureaucracy, and indifference."

What governance structures are needed to provide oversight and perspective along the way? Remember, you are what you measure. How will outside perspective benefit the business strategy? What is the system of controls and oversight being used?

If the intention is to own but not run the business in the future, who is protecting the shareholders? If you need to develop a board, how do you define its mandate, select directors, and run it to add value to the business?

Defining The Role Of Directors
In Private Companies

Strategy has been defined as the art of finding an unfair competitive advantage in the marketplace. It is implemented through defined objectives, plans, and tactics. Whether public or private, driving strategy is how boards create value. Public companies tend to have well-staffed strategy groups, of which M&A is one component. The strategic role of a private company board of directors tends to be simpler.

Private companies with greater than a few hundred million dollars in revenue move along an evolutionary path resembling public company strategy functions. But most private companies are smaller than $100 million in revenue and have no formal strategy function. They are focused on surviving, and hopefully prospering, in a single market.

The goal of a public company is to maximize shareholder value, which today means increasing the stock price. The quarterly treadmill drives behaviors. Private companies are not on the quarterly treadmill, so their strategic horizon is typically much longer than a public company.

The primary functions of a private company board of directors include:

- Strategy
- Oversight
- Succession planning
- Capital structure
- Risk management

Strategy and succession planning are the responsibilities that a board manages to create value, while capital structure and risk management are more often seen as ways to protect the enterprise. Oversight is why the board is considered the "adult in the room."

The Strategic Role Of The Board Of Directors

Private company board strategies should be crafted around answering the question, "What do you want to do with your business?" Private companies do not answer to outside parties, except their lenders and the IRS. Since there are typically only one or two opinions that matter, if the owners are happy, that is good enough.

I submit that effective board strategies can be summed up in the following three questions:

1. What Are The Owners' Goals For The Business?

   Defining the owners' goals usually happens through a visioning exercise: What do you want the company to look like in five years? This usually turns into a desired set of financial statements, some market share and product descriptors, and a few qualitative statements (e.g., "most desired employer").

   There is a well-understood process for moving from a visioning exercise to a full strategic plan to achieve the business' goals. From the board's perspective, such a strategic plan needs to address these questions:

- Does the board have a plan to allocate profits between funding growth, paying down debt, tax distributions, and spendable distributions to owners?
- Are cash balances disproportionately high compared to monthly fixed costs?
- Does the dividend policy meet the needs of the owners?
- Do the external capital sources (the bank) support your capital structure?
- Does management have a strong grip on growth opportunities in adjacent markets?
- Is there an open discussion on how much risk the board and ownership will accept?

If the owners do not have significant experience outside of their business, they may not know they need to comprehensively ask and answer these questions. That is why it is common for outside directors to lead on these issues in a private company board of directors.

2. How Do You Translate The Owners' Goals Into The Budget, Dividend Policy, And Capital Structure?

Many companies have completed thorough strategy exercises that produce a nice report, which is then put on the shelf. If management behavior is not itself managed by the board, market forces will drive management behavior instead. Capital should be allocated to the highest and best uses to achieve the owners' goals. Performance incentives need to support the corporate goals. Setting priorities means killing pet projects outside any private company board strategies designed to usher in success on a larger scale.

Outside directors often need to be the "adult in the room" when forcing the budget to reflect priorities. This usually does not happen naturally.

3. How Do You Measure Progress Toward The Owners' Goals?

Budgets alone are not enough to measure progress in pursuing a strategy. A board needs to develop measurable metrics (e.g., key performance indicators [KPIs], dashboards, etc.) that best speak to progress on strategic imperatives. Budget numbers and financials are not sufficiently indicative for this purpose.

These metrics should be developed with management to assure their full buy-in. A well-run private company board of directors will have an end-to-end process that drives management and staff behavior to fully align with ownership goals, and with accountability set in place.

Good leadership will translate these KPIs from the company level to management performance appraisals, and finally, staff appraisals. They should already be tied to the budget and capital expenditure program. Once developed, these KPIs need to be the live-or-die metrics going forward. This is a primary method for boards to hold management accountable.

Assessing Strategies For Maximum Success

If you serve on a private company's board of directors, you should understand, evaluate, and improve the company strategy. This is one of the ways you demonstrate your value as a director.

If you are considering joining a private company board, you should evaluate the strategic role of the board beforehand to understand how the board functions and its impact on the business.

The transparency of the public markets drives accountability, which is often lacking in private companies. This is where outside directors often make a difference in private company governance.

Advisory Board Styles To Fit Every Business

The boards of directors of for-profit and non-profit organizations have the same fiduciary responsibilities: duty of care, loyalty, and good faith. While like fiduciary boards, advisory boards are not the same. The purpose and function of a board of advisors are usually not as broad as a fiduciary board, but outside advisors should conduct themselves with the same duties in mind.

Advisory boards are the manifestation of each company's needs. The breadth of subjects and depth of discussion varies based on those needs. Advisory boards are usually formed when critical matters are too difficult for owners to handle on their own. Ownership must then solicit outside advice.

The Three Most Common Advisory Boards You'll Encounter

There is one key difference when establishing an advisory board versus a board of directors: there is no regulatory oversight required of advisory board members. In other words, there is no fiduciary duty to the company. This allows for more flexibility in developing governance mechanisms.

Over the years, I have seen advisory boards cluster into three styles:

Consulting Boards. These boards meet one or two days per year (e.g., when there is a pressing issue). The owners buy a day of consulting time from the outside advisors to focus on the issue of the day. Businesses with $20–$50 million in revenue may start with a consulting board before moving up. Businesses under $10 million typically do not have functioning boards.

Junior Advisory Boards. As businesses grow, junior advisory boards pay more attention to the following issues:

- Management depth
- Capital structure
- Long-term planning
- Competition
- Organizational capabilities
- Market structure
- Crisis management (usually involving the bank)

Advisors raise important questions and help solve existential problems. However, the discussions often tiptoe around delicate issues like management performance, compensation, and succession planning.

Full Advisory Boards. This type of board is most comparable to a fiduciary board. Outsiders are actively engaged in succession planning, management compensation, and management performance evaluation. This is more common with companies with several hundred million dollars in revenue because the complexity forces ownership to seek outside help.

At this size, ownership is keenly aware of succession issues. Since there is likely a mix of family and professional management or a transition toward professional managers, succession planning and management training and development are time-consuming subjects for the board.

How To Choose The Right Board Style

How do you know which style is most appropriate? In addition to the needs of the business, the board becomes a reflection of the owners' needs and personalities.

Advisory boards are usually formed when critical matters are too difficult for owners to handle on their own.

If the outside advisors are diligent before accepting, they will understand these constraints before the first meeting. Additionally, as the board's charter expands, so does the drive to seek more professional advisors instead of golf buddies, lawyers, and bankers.

While most businesses strive to grow, their growth rate is typically not so fast that the demands on the board change quickly. (Venture stage businesses are the obvious exception to this statement.) Absent a major change in the business, the type of advisory board is unlikely to change. This catalyst is likely to be a capital event, change in key executives, or exogenous industry event that creates a shockwave or trauma that must urgently be addressed.

Newton's first law of motion states that a body stays in motion unless acted upon by another force. In the same way, owners tend to stay on the same path until the pain of conflict forces them to change. The greater the pain, the greater the need for outside advisors. Therefore, outside advisors should be selected with the experience and judgment proportionate to the need. Businesses in transition need a high-functioning board.

Warren Buffett is famous for his annual letters. There is much a private company owner can learn from him. That also applies to his thoughts about directors. When I read his comments, I try to figure out how to downsize them to work for private companies without the resources and complexities of the companies he owns.

Independent Directors Targeted In Warren Buffett's Annual Letter

Each year, Warren Buffett writes a detailed letter to his investors to share his thoughts on Berkshire's performance and related matters. Warren Buffet's annual letter is one of the most highly anticipated written pieces of the year in the investment community. At fourteen pages, it is different from the usual CEO letter that one finds in a Fortune 500 annual report.

In 2020, he added pointed comments on public company directors; most were not favorable. Having served on twenty-one public boards, Buffett certainly has a perspective to offer his readers regarding independent directors. While laying out his points, he cited examples of how the work used to be done versus how it is done today.

While he did not say it explicitly, we know that some of these negative behaviors occur due to the increasingly litigious nature of business today.

Boards are not supposed to delegate responsibilities to outside professionals. For cautionary tales of why this is true, think about Enron (Andersen 2001), Bernie Madoff (Friehling 2009), WorldCom (Andersen 2002), Refco (E&Y, Grant Thornton), Peregrine Systems (Andersen 2013), or any of the many other financial disasters that had Big Four CPAs and prestigious law firms endorsing the board's actions just before calamity struck.

Key Takeaways On Independent Directors And What Drives The Board

Here were Buffett's concerns with how the position of an independent director has evolved:

1. Compensation for directors confuses incentives and weakens independence.

2. Audit committees need to work harder to avoid CEOs playing numbers games.
3. Compensation committees are increasingly dependent on consultants.
4. Acquisitions tend to be pre-packaged, with little room for debate.

Director Pay. Public company directors are typically paid $250,000 to $300,000. Independent directors are allowed to serve on multiple boards, and some produce $1 million/year of income by sitting on boards. At what point is this about the money, at the expense of duty of care and loyalty? Most private company directors learn quickly: you don't do it for the money. The exception to this is larger private equity portfolio companies. So, this concern does not creep into private company governance easily.

Audit. The quarterly treadmill has long driven CEOs to "beat expectations"—even if only by a penny. This does little for creating long-term value. It creates incentives for CEOs to play games with the financials to earn this year's bonus, sometimes at the expense of long-term shareholder value. Audit committees need to work harder to find out what is buried in the details that may be questionable.

This issue has more to do with ownership directives than CEO behaviors. Quarterly performance is irrelevant to most private companies, but the gamesmanship is real regarding annual bonuses and possible equity incentive structures.

Compensation. Buffett's annual letter also covers compensation. His point is that compensation used to be fair and simple, and now it is complex and causes animosity with outsiders. It is a major point in several presidential campaigns, and for the wrong reasons.

Acquisitions. Rule #1 in acquisitions is don't fall in love with your deal, but this is what is happening. The presentations are pre-packaged for board review, so instead of inviting productive dissent and debate, they squash contrary opinions. Why is this in the owners' interest? Most acquisitions fail, so why do companies keep doing them?

Executive Sessions. On the plus side, the mandated executive sessions are welcomed in Buffett's annual letter. This provides a time for the independent directors to have a frank conversation about the CEO's performance, with the CEO not in the room.

While all these issues plague public companies, most private companies do not suffer from these problems. But private companies are at risk. What drives public company boards usually trickles down and morphs into negative forces for private companies, albeit at a smaller scale.

Are your outside directors and advisors up to the challenge of remaining truly independent? Even with independent directors, for a business to endure for decades, the leadership needs to expect and plan for the unexpected. A system of risk management will help your company do just that.

Creating A Risk Management System

Most business owners are so busy running their business that they don't have time to think about unlikely events. How can you think about possible "black swan events" when you struggle with today's problems? To protect shareholders, boards and management need to think about the causes, frequency, and severity of unusual events.

Unlike an investment, which drives revenue or reduces costs, risk management programs are not just about the numbers. It is easier to justify an investment when you can measure the benefit. It is hard to write a check for something unlikely to happen. Consider the difference between buying insurance, backup generators, or cyber defenses when you want to spend more on marketing and sales.

The key drivers in risk management are risk tolerance and judgment. These vary widely from person to person. A management team may be cohesive and high-perform-ing, but that does not mean each person has the same risk tolerance.

How To Best Examine Business Risks

In a recent situation, the outside directors lead the board through an exercise to define, qualify, rate, and rank the major threats to the business. These risks included regula-tory changes, supplier pressures, natural disasters, cyber, key man, and technology risks. The individual executives had a good grasp of their view of risk, but they had never discussed it as a management team. So, while there were a lot of well-formed opinions, there was not a consolidated view, and therefore no action plan. Without a consolidated view, the company could not define the costs and risk/reward of investing in protective measures. They could not develop a risk management plan.

Step 1: What Are The Risks? For this company, the first step was to separate insurable from uninsurable risks. The insurable risks had been handled consistently and responsibly by the CFO. The board reviewed the program and agreed that most of it was appropriate but wanted to spend more time understanding cyber coverage. Since this is a rapidly evolving area, this effort was needed. (See the chart on the next page.)

The harder part was to define, rate, and rank the intangible risks to the business. This is a classic case of the value being in the process; considerable debate and head-scratching were needed to produce a simplistic-looking outcome.

Over a series of board meetings, and with committee meetings in between, the directors debated the risks across the enterprise and within individual lines of business.

Step 2: Continuing Management Of Risks. Establishing a risk management plan is not enough; it must be continuously managed. The second step is the ongoing monitoring and course corrections needed to keep the risk management system current. Each quarter, the board takes a deeper dive into one or two specific issues. For a year, each major risk is thoroughly vetted. Budgets can be set and adjusted based on changing conditions and risk tolerance.

Enterprise Risk Assessment

		Enterprise Risk			
		Severity of Risk	Likelihood of Risk	Preparedness to Mitigate the Risk	Comments
Please rate each Enterprise Risk on Three Dimensions: - Severity of the risk - Likelihood of the risk - Preparedness to mitigate the risk		4. 3. 2. 1.	5. 4. 3. 2. 1.	3. 2. 1.	
Top Enterprise Risks	1. Management Risks				
	2. Competitive Risks				
	3.Supplier Risks				
	4.Regulatory Risks				
	5. Technology Risks				
	6. Environmental Risks				

Severity of Risk
4. May impact the long-term viability of the business
3. May significantly impact the margins of the business over the long-term
2.May significantly impact the short-term financial health of the business
1. May impact the short-term financial health of the business

Likelihood of Risk
5. Extremely likely / Will happen
4. Very likely
3. Somewhat likely
2. Not very likely
1. Not likely at all

Preparedness to Mitigate the Risk
3. We do not understand this risk the way we should and need to devote more time and resources preparing
2. We need to improve our preparation for this risk and/or devote more resources to mitigating this risk
1. We understand and are prepared for this risk and should not devote more resources unless something changes

Family and other private businesses still have a fiduciary duty to their shareholders, even if they are key executives or minor children. The duty of care is a prime responsibility for all fiduciary directors, regardless of ownership structure. Managing risk is the essence of the duty of care for directors.

Make sure you and your directors establish a risk management plan that addresses all the potential risks and threats to your business. If you are diligent about the process, your company will be protected for years to come.

Designing A Board That Can Pull Your Business Through Crisis

The COVID-19 crisis was unlike anything we've seen before. Not only is this pandemic unprecedented, but it's also having a different impact on different industries. While some organizations have been forced to a near standstill, others are forced to increase productivity under pressure to survive. One item remains constant: having a seasoned board is more important now than ever before.

While there is no one-size-fits-all solution to assembling an exceptional board, even exceptional businesses need one. However, most private companies do not have functioning boards.

Having served as an outside director on numerous boards during periods of crisis, I believe that assembling the right board is like finding the right pair of shoes. You need a good fit with the right degree of support and responsiveness to accomplish your goals. Just as you would hike the Appalachian Trail in different shoes than you'd choose to run the

Boston Marathon, the right board enables your business' optimal agility across industry-specific terrain.

It's never too late to assemble the best possible board. If this pandemic has taught us anything, it's that the next black swan event is always on the horizon and learning from the current crisis is the first step to preparing for the next crisis.

Here are some ideas to help form or restructure your company's board right now.

It's important to understand different types of boards and how they may benefit your business. While public companies are required to have boards, private companies are only required to on paper. Owners often wait until their business faces an unforeseen hurdle that forces them to seek outside help. The higher the hurdle, the more perspective is needed to clear it. For troubled businesses, the more your business is hurting, the more you need a board. For high-growth businesses, the board can help to evaluate opportunities so you pursue those with the highest and best use of time, talent, and capital.

A board of directors with fiduciary responsibilities is different from an advisory board. A board of directors is responsible for governance, oversight, financial management, risk management, and management succession. Though advisory boards may perform similar functions, they have no fiduciary duty to the company, and therefore have flexibility in how they're assembled. There are three common types of advisory boards.

Consulting boards, usually for businesses with under $50 million in revenue, meet irregularly to address temporally pressing issues. Growing businesses may graduate to junior advisory boards, which consistently address more existential issues related to market structure, long-term planning, and crisis management. Companies with hundreds of millions in revenue ultimately require full advisory boards, which intervene on even more complex issues, such as succession planning and performance evaluation.

Private and family business owners are often tempted to seek sporadic and informal advice from personal friends, lawyers, and bankers. These types of boards may suffice for a time, but a major catalyst like a capital event or sudden executive change—not to mention a global pandemic—will almost always reveal them to be insufficient.

The right board will ultimately become a big driver in the value of your business because it functions to protect the business as an asset. The right governance solution for your business may not have or even need all the bells and whistles, but it does have the core values of objectivity, oversight, and complementary expertise. Businesses with appropriate governance do better than businesses that go it alone.

The Art Of Designing A Board

Because even a full board cannot include every conceivable skill and expertise, selecting the best possible board is an art. This requires establishing the seats you need to fill first, then recruiting the best-fit candidates. Sometimes, CEOs become enamored with a personality first, then try to fit that personality on the board; these scenarios rarely result in long-term success.

Board members must be able to maintain objectivity in all circumstances; this is their primary responsibility. Your board will quickly lose its effectiveness if members cannot offer their honest opinions. A good board member can tactfully disagree with ownership and offer alternative solutions without fear of being replaced. They have mastered the art of disagreeing without being disagreeable.

Though assembling a board requires careful thought and insight, there is a relatively simple litmus test for its sustainability: in a well-functioning board, colleagues can have a visceral disagreement, then immediately look forward to going out to lunch with each other.

How Boards Navigate Crises

One of a board's most valuable functions is navigating crises. Different voices and opinions naturally have a stabilizing effect. They yield more rational thought and reduce panic. They also bring a diversity of knowledge, experiences, and resources to the table. Since crises like COVID-19 often affect management personally, boards are responsible for preventing emotion from clouding sound business judgment.

As management focuses on handling short-term logistical adaptations to issues such as social distancing regulations and supply chain disruptions, boards should keep the business' long-term mission in sight. A board should be able to preserve a business' competitive advantage through digital transformation and customer experience initiatives while monitoring industry competition—even as management is still busy putting out fires.

Having a diverse board with at least one member who has crisis management experience is vital. Though COVID-19 resists comparison to past catastrophes in many ways, members who have navigated events such as 9/11 and the 2008 financial crisis have experience overcoming uncertainty which is valuable during any black swan event.

Your board members should have accumulated enough battle scars to say, "Here's what we have learned in the past. Here's what you need to think about now and into the future." You want your company's board to be filled with people you know who will be able to handle the unknown because they've done it before.

Use Good Governance To Steer A Rudderless Ship

Much like in the public equity markets, singular unexpected events can greatly increase or destroy the value of a private company. Even the most thoughtful business continuity planning will fail to anticipate every scenario. The unexpected death of a strong-willed founder is a frequent example. Most private companies do not have well-developed succession plans, especially when the long-term owner and founder may focus more on their lifestyle than the business.

A well-functioning board should be able to manage this scenario. When in doubt, the board is in charge. But what happens when there is no board? Who steers the ship? A recent experience highlights how good governance can help even in the most difficult situations.

A global technology company enjoyed thirty-five years of growth and prosperity. The organization included dozens of offices around the world. Many of its clients were household names. A single owner had built the company and a few loyal lieutenants into a $500-million-revenue business. But the business revolved around the owner, a true entrepreneur. The same owner had failed to do any succession planning. So, when he died unexpectedly, the business became a rudderless ship. The equity passed to a trust for the benefit of the owner's minor children. The trustee was the owner's estate attorney, who had no practical business experience and was quickly overwhelmed.

A family confidant introduced me to the trustee. It was clear that the trustee could not define and prioritize the issues needed to execute his duties.

After a few discussions, I suggested this plan of action:

- The trustee had exposure as the sole director and as a trustee. He needed to review his legal and fiduciary responsibilities with his counsel and insurance carriers and assess his various liability insurance policies to ensure they were adequate for the risks he was bearing.
- He needed to establish a protocol for interacting with the young beneficiaries to represent their interests.

- The bylaws were written thirty-five years ago for a single-member LLC. They were antiquated and grossly insufficient for the current and future situation. The bylaws needed to be rewritten with governance best practices for a global company with outside directors.
- The company's D&O and other policies would need to be revised to attract the outside directors needed.
- The company needed to reassure its banks and major creditors that it would be stable during the transition period. Since there was no CEO, the trustee and remaining management would need to step in and make this happen.
- Outside directors were needed to bring the experience, judgment, and decisiveness the trustee lacked. We established a search process and found three excellent candidates. Since the trustee had no experience in search work, we managed the search, set compensation, and onboarded the new directors.
- Once the directors were elected, we shifted into phase two, making the board operational. The board needed a chair other than the trustee because the trustee did not want to be conflicted with his duty to the trust. The chairperson then created an agenda process to manage the short-term crisis and create a regular order for the board's business.
- The next step was to establish the governance, compensation, and audit committees. The outside directors used their prior experience to get these

committees up and running quickly.
- Three things became clear:
    - The trust wanted to sell the business but was not in a rush and would wait to get the best outcome.
    - The company needed to hire a CEO fit for the situation.
    - No one was in charge until the new CEO started about six to nine months later.

This forced the board to grapple with a new reality: It could not wait for a new CEO to address major staff and competitive issues, yet there were no worthy internal candidates to bridge the gap. Should they hire a consultant to step in and risk possible management defections? Or should one of the board members step in, on an interim basis, to provide the sorely lacking leadership? The latter is what we did, and what I would advise you to do in a similar situation.

Work Quickly. When the owner died, competitors spread rumors of financial problems to undermine the company's stellar reputation. Employees worried about the company's health, and competitors started luring key employees. Time can be against you after a sudden change in your business, so get to work right away.

Analyze Your Options. Working with the remaining management team, we quickly conducted a SWOT (strengths, weaknesses, opportunities, threats) analysis and assessed unit managers' capabilities. We identified several major growth opportunities that would be missed if we waited another year. The business had been undermanaged for many years, and this inquiry revealed a strong, vital company culture looking to charge forward. When making major changes at such a pivotal time, look at all your options before determining the next steps.

Adapt To The Circumstances

One of my recommendations was for one of the directors with experience stepping in on an interim basis to guide the business before smoothly transitioning leadership to the new CEO. While ordinarily, this would violate the board's oversight responsibilities, these were not ordinary times. The board debated and defined the scope of the role, so there was no confusion on the transition process to the new CEO. Remember that good governance also means adapting to short-term needs.

When a sudden and potentially catastrophic event happens, work fast to mitigate the negative effects. Give the management team and employees the security they need to focus on their jobs. Do whatever you can to keep clients from being negatively impacted. Finally, position the company to get back into growth mode. As a result, everyone's interests can be well-served.

The next task is to plan for management succession, a subject examined in the following chapter.

Your Ownership Journey

Secret #6. Assess And Develop
Proper Governance

» Governance is the bridge between ownership and management. It is best served by independent thinkers not distracted by personal agendas.

» Board members must maintain objectivity in all circumstances; this is their primary responsibility.

» Strategy and succession planning are the responsibilities that a board manages to create value, while capital structure and risk management are more often seen as ways to protect the enterprise. Oversight is why the board is considered the "adult in the room."

» While public companies are required to have boards, most private companies do not have functioning or effective boards.

» Advisory boards are usually formed when critical matters are too difficult for owners to handle on their own.

» Boards of directors have fiduciary responsibilities: duty of care, loyalty, and good faith. Although like fiduciary boards, the duties of an advisory board are defined by the ownership that creates it and may be limited or non-existent.

Plan For Management Succession

Management succession is a $1 trillion a year problem.

In a 2021 issue of the *Harvard Business Review*, Claudio Fernández-Aráoz, an executive fellow for executive education at Harvard Business School, and two co-authors examined "The High Cost of Poor Succession Planning."[12]

> *According to our analysis, the amount of market value wiped out by badly managed CEO and C-suite transitions in the S&P 1500 is close to $1 trillion a year. … Why are some of the world's biggest and most powerful organizations getting CEO appointments so wrong? For five main reasons: lack of attention to succession, poor leadership development, suboptimal board composition, lazy hiring practices, and conflicted search firms.*

If big business struggles with management succession, imagine the problems at small to midsize companies.

One of the biggest mistakes business owners can make is not identifying future leadership needs. Evaluating internal candidates, completing a gap analysis, and outlining transition plans are all important steps to ensure the business has strong leadership into the foreseeable future.

Creating Momentum In Your Succession Planning Process

When taking on a new succession planning assignment, I always ask clients to do some homework to prepare themselves for what lies ahead. I advise them that there are separate and parallel paths for planning business succession versus ownership succession. The latter tends to revolve around personal wants and needs and is more subjective.

The planning process is a bit like blazing a path through a dense jungle. You have a sense of where you want to go, but you can't see far ahead of where you are, and the footing is hazardous. So, you take a step or two, reassess your position, and think about the next few steps. There is rarely a straight path forward, and you progress in fits and starts, depending on the issues of the moment.

Creating A Plan: Business Issues

To acquaint them with the issues, I ask clients to write out the answers to these questions:

1. What is the state of the business today? How healthy is it? It is important to be realistic about what you own and control. This discussion will anchor the process going forward.
2. What are the industry issues that ownership cannot control and must accept? Do you have a firm grip on your competitive position? Your industry fundamentals likely control your growth rate and profitability.

3. What is the growth potential of the business? What might a new owner do with the business? When you look to exit ownership, you need to look at the business as a new owner. What are they likely to want to do with it? Why do they want your business?
4. What investment may be needed to maximize the growth potential? That includes people, money, technology, real estate, partnerships, etc. What investment will the new owner need to make to achieve the potential you envision? How does that impact how you market the asset?

The business issues are more numerical and fact-based. They are discussed every day with the management team, customers, and suppliers.

Creating A Plan: Personal Issues

Business issues are usually easier to wrestle with because they are about the everyday work that you do. But assessing your wants and needs as an owner can be challenging, circular, and sometimes frustrating.

If you are both owner and CEO, then you will be asking these questions to yourself. If you have a professional management team, you need to tell them about your expectations of them.

1. What are your personal goals (financial, lifestyle, family, health, philanthropy)? This question is often the hardest and needs the most consideration. There is no reason to rush it and no reason to think there is only one right answer.

2. What are the issues and concerns of your family? If you have a family business, what are the family issues you need to contend with in your exit planning? Yes, this may be a tough one. If you are struggling, a family business consultant may be needed to deal with family issues.

3. What are the business and personal risks that need to be weighed? What risks are you unwilling to accept? At some point, you know what you can't tolerate. So, it is better to identify the no-go situations upfront and use those constraints to find a path forward.

Setting Priorities

When you put these pieces together, do clear priorities present themselves? If the path forward is still murky, you may need to work harder to define, clarify, and understand the issues. Keep working on the issues until priorities come into focus.

How do we translate these priorities into specific scenarios and action plans? What are the pros, cons, and risks of each scenario?

Once you have a set of business and personal priorities, get out your machete and start marching through the jungle. As in a movie, keep the group together, and beware of quicksand and other threats—they could be anywhere. Trust your instincts and follow the data.

Driving The Action Plan

Unlike a jungle safari, you can have reasonable visibility when planning your succession process. In the jungle, it is unsafe to stay in one place too long; it is usually better to keep moving.

The analogy in business is that not making a decision is a decision, and it usually winds up being a bad one. It is usually better to decide and if it doesn't look good, adjust the course based on what you learned. This is like agile programming in software.

So, what is your time frame for action? When do you have to, or should you, make a decision, even if you are not completely comfortable with the outcomes?

In business school, I was taught that the ultimate act of leadership was to replace oneself, making the successor successful and taking oneself out of the spotlight. That is the sum of the succession planning process: You are doing tough work to benefit others, not yourself. That is the sign of a leader.

How To Plan For Management Succession

One of the most basic responsibilities of a board of directors or advisors is to provide for management succession. Emergencies tend to resolve themselves since decisions must be made and cannot be delayed.

Proactive management succession planning is the hallmark of a well-run organization. More than thinking about who the next CEO will be, how do you develop the layers of direct reports which will be pulled up the organization chart or moved aside?

It all starts with deciding where you want the organization to go, understanding the requirements of the leadership positions to get there, and working backward from there. If you don't know where you are going, how do you know when you get there?

This chart maps out the overall process.

Business Objectives Drive Talent Needs

Understanding your future talent requirements means identifying the overall business deliverables and assigning components to specific positions. From there, you need to deduce the skills and experiences needed to achieve those goals. Success is usually determined by cultural fit, style, and experience.

Assessing the current staff needs to include their interpersonal skills and cultural fit for the mission ahead, regardless of the past. Do they align with the business vision? Can you quantify past performance with data, or is it just opinions and biases? Were the performance appraisals thoroughly and fairly written?

The Skill/Will Matrix is a quick and simple tool to assess your current talent. Developed in the 1970s, it segments people by their expertise and their desire to be successful. Each quadrant requires different types of supervision and development.

The new positions under review need to be ranked and rated, meaning new job descriptions need to be written and rated for market compensation levels. For your current staff, what development do they need to get there—to have the skills and experience to be successful? Otherwise, you need to go outside.

Once you have decided where you are headed, determined the skills and experiences for leaders to get you there, and considered your current staff, complete a gap analysis. What is the difference between what you need and what you have? With development, can the internal candidates meet the need? If not, go outside to fill the positions.

Transition timelines should be developed in detail since, at this point, management succession is about project management. If you don't identify the details, assign duties and deadlines, and track them religiously, time will slip, and it may not happen.

Developing the timelines often means working backward from an immovable deadline, such as a planned retirement. When does the candidate need to be in the new job and fully up to speed? How long will it take to train them and backfill their current position? How long will it take to recruit and onboard the backfilled positions? When do you have to start this chain of events?

It is important to start with an honest assessment of your business, its governance, and yourself. Dealing with potential conflicts early and directly is usually best, as these things do not get better on their own.

Since this impacts people's careers and livelihoods, thoughtful communication is critical. Who needs to know what and when without creating a rumor mill? Certainly, the beneficiaries need to be brought along early. But people likely to be disappointed with the results need to be treated with dignity and respect.

Identify Your Business Objectives To Determine Management Succession Needs

A primary responsibility of a board of directors is to provide management continuity. Emergencies tend to resolve themselves since decisions cannot wait. Proactive management succession planning is the hallmark of a well-run organization and is more demanding than pondering who the next CEO will be.

Your business strategy drives your future leadership requirements. Then, work backward to build the succession plan.

If you do not know where you are going, how do you know how to get there?

Understanding your future talent requirements means identifying the future business objectives and designing the organization to get there. From there, you need to:

Consider the skills and experiences needed to achieve those goals. Success is usually determined by cultural fit, style, and experience.

Realize that filling positions is often a trade-off between *must-haves* **and** *wanna-haves***.** The pivot is typically made when you decide what you can and cannot live without.

Assess the current staff needs to include their interpersonal skills and cultural fit regardless of the past. Do they align with the business vision? Can you quantify past performance with data, or is it just a collection of biased opinions? Were the past performance appraisals thorough and fair?

Figuring Out What You Need

In your future organization, there are likely new positions to be created and new job descriptions to be written and rated for compensation purposes. For your current staff, what development do they need to acquire the skills and experience to fill those roles? If you lack the internal talent needed to staff the future organization, you need to go outside.

You need to complete a gap analysis once you've:

1. Decided where you are headed
2. Discovered the skills and experiences leaders must possess to achieve your business objectives
3. Evaluated your current staff

The gap analysis should involve these questions:

1. What is the difference between what you need and what you have?
2. With development, can the internal candidates meet future expectations? If not, then you need to go outside to fill the gaps.

Management Succession Timelines

Transition timelines should be developed, in detail, since at this point, management succession tends to mean applying thorough project management skills. If you do not identify the details, assign duties and deadlines, and track them religiously, time will slip, and a smooth succession may not happen or happen on time.

Developing the timelines often means working backward from an immovable deadline, such as a planned retirement. When does the candidate need to be in the new job and fully up to speed? How long will it take to train them and backfill their current position? How long will it take to recruit and onboard the backfilled positions? When do you have to start this chain of events?

Thoughtful Communication

It is important to start with an honest assessment of your business, its governance, and yourself.

Dealing with potential conflicts early and directly is usually best, as these things do not get better independently.

Management succession is both a process and a project to be managed. It takes time and energy and should not be rushed. Give yourself enough time to figure it out and likely three to five years to execute.

Why Succession Planning Is Vital

COVID-19 drastically altered the course of America's small and midsize businesses (SMBs). According to a 2020 Facebook survey of over 86,000 small and midsize owners, managers, and employees, about one-third of SMBs are closed. Nearly half of the owners whose businesses are still open are suffering burnout. Fewer than half of nonoperational SMBs plan to rehire the same workers, and over a third of operational SMBs have shifted exclusively to e-commerce.[13]

A 2018 survey from Wilmington Trust of two hundred privately held business owners revealed that 58 percent do not have a succession plan, even though long-term transition planning has yielded better business outcomes. Though "getting older" is the most oft-cited impetus for establishing a succession plan, 47 percent of business owners over the age of sixty-five still don't have one.[14]

During the pandemic, never was the value of comprehensive succession planning so apparent. Even the best plan cannot predict a global crisis. But it can certainly help preserve a family's financial interests and its delicate relationship dynamics.

It's not too late to begin succession planning. Here is some distilled wisdom to help you get started as soon as possible.

Work On Your Business

An old trope says family business owners must wear three hats—owner, boss, and employee. Depending on which hat they're wearing, owners either work in the business or on the business.

One of the key issues to understand when you own and manage your own business is the difference between working on the business versus working in the business (a concept popularized by Michael Gerber in his teachings on The E-Myth[15]). While most of your time is spent working in the business, the high-impact decisions you will make pertain to working on the business. Oddly, the time spent on these decisions is typically inverse to their importance.

When working in a business, it's easy to get so caught up in everyday operations that you don't have a chance to ask yourself how you're leveraging the business as an asset.

Working on a business requires owners to break from the daily grind of sixty- to eighty-hour workweeks to ask questions like:

- *How can this business improve my life?*
- *What is the state of the industry?*
- *Should I take more or less risk?*
- *How should I capitalize my business?*
- *Should I make an acquisition or sell some/all of my business?*

It can be hard for an owner to shift from working in to working on their business because they often form an emotional attachment as if the business was their child. But a business is an asset, not a child. Getting clear about this distinction is the first step in strong succession planning.

Consider Risk Versus Reward

An owner's most important decisions are made when working on their business. From this perspective, owners are better able to objectively analyze their preconceived ideas. For example, many view their family business as their birthright, intended to be passed from generation to generation.

Many have been conditioned to measure their success as the difference between what they inherited and what they passed down to their children. But the idea of a family business as a birthright is inherently flawed because it doesn't account for how industries change (and sometimes completely transform) over twenty or thirty years.

Protecting the future financial health of your family requires objectively looking at the state of your industry today and for the next decade. Is your industry in growth or consolidation mode? How risky will it be to continue to own the business now and into the near-term horizon?

Your agenda as an owner is to decide how much capital to deploy, how much risk to take, what business you are in, and who is responsible for running the business. If your business becomes unacceptably risky, ask yourself why you want to own the business—then examine your answer. If much of your business' value is attached to you being the CEO, consider the impact your absence would have.

Seek Objective Facilitation

It's almost impossible for families to rationally evaluate their businesses without objective third-party facilitation. Owners who are excellent at running their businesses might not see the need for facilitation. But business ownership can be like homeownership; even though you can do many things by yourself, sometimes you need to hire an expert. For example, you probably always want to hire a professional electrician—otherwise, you might get hurt.

Everyone can benefit from a facilitator because we all have biases that can hinder objective and effective decision-making. Facilitation helps families create an environment where they can take off their everyday hats and look at the facts through a clearer lens. A good facilitator will constructively challenge the thinking of everyone involved in succession planning.

Depending on the dexterity and maturity of an owner and their family, they may need a lot or a little facilitation. A business composed of a father and two sons might be more emotionally challenging than a business with five or ten active family members asking constructive questions.

Leadership can be lonely. A great leadership challenge is that no one tells you what decisions to make and when— especially when confronting your mortality through succession planning. But for an experienced facilitator, succession planning isn't personal. Precisely because a facilitator is not your family, they can ultimately be your family's strongest ally.

But what happens when problems arise? And they will arise. That is when you need to use effective conflict resolution and mediation, which will be examined in the following chapter.

Your Ownership Journey

Secret #7. Plan For Management Succession

» Not making a decision is a decision, and it usually winds up being a bad one.

» Succession planning is the biggest risk for most private companies.

» There should be separate and parallel paths for planning management succession and ownership succession.

» Proactive management succession planning is the hallmark of a well-run organization. More than thinking about who the next CEO will be, how do you develop the layers of direct reports which will be pulled up the organization chart or moved aside?

» Since succession planning impacts people's careers and livelihoods, thoughtful communication is critical. Who needs to know what and when without creating a rumor mill?

» A good facilitator will constructively challenge the thinking of everyone involved in succession planning.

Utilize Conflict Resolution And Mediation To Build Effective Relationships

Consider this legal adage: when it comes to conflicts, clients should understand it is to their benefit to trade hope for certainty.

Conflicts are a part of the history of America. George Washington was not only a great military leader and president, but he was also a shrewd person when it came to conflict resolution. In his will, Washington set out a structure for resolution if a dispute should arise after his passing.

All disputes (if unhappily any should arise) shall be decided by three impartial and intelligent men known for their probity and understanding; two to be chosen by the disputants, each having the choice of one, and the third by those two—which three men thus chosen, shall unfettered by law, or legal constructions, declare their sense of the Testator's intention; and such decision is, to all intents and purposes to be as binding on the parties as if it had been given in the Supreme Court of the United States.

Identifying and managing conflict is a necessary evil for any business owner, and many tools exist to assist with that process. I think it's important to distinguish between managing conflicts within an organization and managing conflicts within an ownership group. For instance:

- Case 1—Your VP of sales and VP of production can't agree on a forecast and have locked horns. Everyone who owns a business has to deal with employees who don't get along, but they need to play nice together to make money.
- Case 2—My brother wants to sell the business and cash out since he doesn't work here, but I want to keep the business since it is my job and how I identify myself to the world. This drives directly to governance, Secret #6, since good governance provides the ownership tools to resolve conflict when formal tools fail.

Conflicts are more dramatic in family businesses since intra-family conflicts are not resolved by legal mechanisms. People must communicate, evaluate, and compromise, and that is difficult when emotions are running high. You can take your business partner to court to resolve a business dispute, and once the judge rules, it is over, and you move on. But you can't take a father, mother, brother, or sister to court for hurting your feelings or treating you poorly.

Let's start with some basics about conflict resolution and then add a layer to address family conflicts. A few case studies will help to reinforce the takeaways for this chapter.

Five Ways To Manage Conflict In The Workplace

By Dan McCarthy

Many people head in the opposite direction when they spot conflict in the workplace. But if you're a manager, that's a mistake. Conflict can be healthy or unhealthy, but either way, it merits your attention.

The healthy conflict focuses on differences of opinion regarding tasks or work-related activities. It can be leveraged and facilitated for gain. Unhealthy conflict is a kind that gets personal. It must be extinguished immediately, or it jeopardizes the work environment.

Five Styles Of Conflict Management

The research work of Kenneth Thomas and Ralph Kilmann in the 1970s led to the identification of five styles of conflict and the development of a widely used self-assessment called the Thomas Kilmann Conflict Mode Instrument, or TKI. Their work suggested that we all have a preferred way to deal with conflict, which serves us well in some situations, but not all. The key to success is to develop a flexible toolkit of conflict management approaches and use the one that best fits the situation.

The more you can get comfortable with each way of dealing with conflict, the more effective you will be.

Collaborating

In the collaborative approach, the manager works with the people involved to develop a win-win solution. The focus is on finding a solution that meets everyone's needs.

This style is appropriate when:

- The situation is not urgent
- An important decision needs to be made
- The conflict involves many people or a few people across teams
- Previous conflict resolution attempts have failed

This style is not appropriate when:

- A decision needs to be made urgently
- The matter is trivial to all involved

Competing

With a competitive approach, the person who takes the firmest stand wins. This style is often seen as aggressive and can cause others in the conflict to feel taken advantage of.

Nevertheless, this style is appropriate when:

- A decision needs to be made quickly
- An unpopular decision needs to be made
- Someone is trying to take advantage of a situation

This style is not appropriate when:

- People are feeling sensitive about the issue
- The situation is not urgent
- Buy-in is important

Compromising

With the compromising approach, each person gives up something that contributes toward conflict resolution.

This style is appropriate when:

- A decision needs to be made sooner rather than later
- Resolving the conflict is more important than having each individual win
- Power among the people in the conflict is equal

This style is not appropriate when:

- A variety of important needs must be met
- The situation is extremely urgent
- One person holds more power than another

Accommodating

The accommodating style is one of the most passive conflict resolution methods. One of the individuals gives in so that the other person can get what they want. As a rule, this style is not effective, but it is appropriate in certain scenarios:

- Maintaining the relationship is more important than winning
- The issue at hand is very important to only one person

This style is not appropriate when:

- It will not permanently solve the problem

Avoiding

The last approach is to avoid conflict entirely. People who use this style tend to accept decisions without question, avoid confrontation, and delegate difficult decisions and tasks. Avoiding is another passive approach that is typically not effective, but it has its uses.

This style is appropriate when:

- The issue is trivial
- The conflict will resolve itself on its own soon

This style is not appropriate when:

- The issue is important to you or your team
- The conflict will grow worse without attention

The Bottom Line

There is no right or wrong style of conflict resolution. Each has its time and place. Learn how to use all five, and you'll be much more effective. As a manager, learn to suggest different approaches based on these five styles to defuse conflict.

Dan McCarthy wrote about management and leadership for The Balance Careers. McCarthy is an expert in leadership and management development. For over twenty years, he has helped thousands of leaders improve their leadership capabilities. As the owner of Great Leadership, he works with organizations and individuals to optimize their leadership capabilities.

How To Manage Conflict In Family Enterprise

Doug Baumoel in *Family Business* magazine presents an interesting three-principle approach to managing conflict:

- Principle #1: Bargaining
- Principle #2: Force
- Principle #3: Development

Once the sources of conflict have been identified and broken down into their constituent parts, "Matching the appropriate approach to each component is critical," Baumoel says.[16]

1. Bargaining
Conventional dispute-resolution techniques, such as direct negotiation and mediation, may effectively address economic issues of money, power, and control. However, one cannot bargain the values of affection, talent, and commitment—nor history. Bargaining is effective only for negotiating specific goals and deciding how decisions are made.

2. Force
Any attempt to force an outcome to one's advantage through the use of power (i.e., litigation or threats of retaliation) runs the risk of exacerbating the conflict. After all, if a conflict is triggered by the disrespected use of power, any additional use of power to manage is likely to make matters worse. As with bargaining, whatever the motivation for using power may be, it can address only issues of opposing goals and how decisions are made. Feelings, history, talent, and psychological issues do not respond to force.

3. Development
While not a term usually associated with managing conflict, development—both structural and personal—can be the most effective approach to managing the systemic conflict that is unique to a family enterprise. It is especially effective when continuing relationships matter. Development is the process of identifying deficiencies and improving them.

For a deeper dive into the topic, I recommend reading Baumoel's entire article.[16]

Bargaining and force are natural ways to deal with conflict. They are akin to the flight, fight, or freeze response that is hardwired into each of us. When animals perceive a threat, their hormonal response takes over. Here is how it is demonstrated in the workplace:

- Fight: "He said what? I am going to fix him."
- Flight: "I don't want to talk to Joe about this; he is going to get angry."
- Freeze: "I can't believe that I told Tom how poorly he is doing, and he might lose his job, but he just sat there and stared at me."

So, while fight/flight/freeze is our default, development is a different way forward. Development means identifying deficiencies in experience, education, or other personal or professional attributes and working to improve them to reduce conflict.

If the participants can grow and expand their thinking beyond instinct, it may create other ways to resolve the conflict besides flight, fight, or freeze.

An idiom, "Before you judge someone, walk a mile in their shoes," suggests being empathetic even in a dispute. As with all negotiations, you need to start by understanding the other person's point of view to be fully informed.

When trying to mediate conflict, I quickly assess the root cause and assess if development is a realistic option, how long it will take, and if there is enough time to try it before emotions hijack the resolution process. If development is a realistic option, I invest in that before employing other methods to resolve the conflict.

Non-Family Conflict

When resolving conflicts between non-family business partners, I focus on agreements, economics, and ego.

What did the parties already agree to, and are they abiding by their agreements? Is there a disagreement because the bylaws did not anticipate this type of situation? Or is one of the parties not doing what they had previously agreed to do because they don't like it anymore? Or does it cost more than they thought it would?

These are facts, not opinions, and it is always best to set the facts straight at the beginning.

Step one is to get everyone back to what was agreed upon and try to enforce it. If the circumstances require the documents to be renegotiated, that may be a worthwhile option.

The second issue, economics, is important to understand before walking in to negotiate. Who gains and loses, and how much? Does everyone understand the impact, or are their calculations faulty? How significant is the impact to the person taking the hit? What if they aren't financially literate and don't know what to ask? This is where I often ask, "Is this the hill you want to die on?"

This is a good example of how development may change a conflict. Getting people to understand the numbers may make it easier to resolve a conflict or motivate them to fight harder since they understand how much they have to lose.

I don't know that I have seen a conflict successfully resolved without comprehending the egos and personalities involved. The sparring parties typically know each other well. They know how to push "hot buttons" to draw a reaction.

If both parties want to get past the conflict, they will understand that any small satisfaction achieved by "getting" the other guy usually comes at a great cost to their business and personal interests. This point is more likely to get lost in family conflicts since so many layers of emotions and long histories are carried into every dispute.

Family Conflict

Family conflicts originate from insufficient communications and conflicts in values.

These conflicts are complicated because they may disagree on business issues, but there are likely communications challenges, which inhibit them from addressing the business issues.

For example, most dads don't walk around saying "I love you" to their adult sons, while at the same time, the sons seek approval and affirmation. Resentment and frustration may build. So rather than discussing the father/son relationship, they spar over business issues. But if they could resolve the father/son relationship, or at least establish boundaries between family and business, then it should become easier to talk about the business issues.

Successful families tend to have sufficient communication (which can be far from ideal) and have consistent values. The black sheep of the family will tend to be an outlier on one of these two vectors.

Let's enumerate the types of dynamics where there is a conflict of values:

- Dad works sixty to seventy hours per week, including weekends, but the son leaves at 3:00 p.m. to play golf a few days per week.
- Dad never met a risk he wouldn't take and had numerous wild goose chases that ended up losing money. The children become conservative and don't take risks.
- Personal styles matter as well. One family person may not be loyal to their marriage or may use company assets for personal gain. These conflict with other family members' values and interests.

Values are easy to identify, typically challenging to discuss, and almost always hard to change without great incentives.

For this reason, try to focus on behaviors, not values, where possible. If you can negotiate behaviors to an acceptable level so that you don't have to try to change the person, it is more likely to come to an acceptable arrangement within the family.

For example, Mom may say, "I can't stop you from doing that, but if you are going to do it, don't do it anywhere around here where any of our friends, family, and staff may find out about it." This is why they say, "What happens in Vegas, stays in Vegas."

Let's look at a handful of cases and then try to draw out lessons that repeat themselves too often:

- The third-generation adult children work together but are in constant battle. Things have come to blows. They are still angry about who got the bicycle in third grade, even though they are now approaching age sixty.
- It is Mom's second marriage and Dad's first. Mom has two adult children from her first marriage, whom Dad has agreed to bring into his business. The older son has been stealing and abusing employees, and the younger son lacks talent but wants to be CEO. Dad loves Mom, and Mom loves her kids, so Dad doesn't say anything since Mom will not allow anything negative to happen to her kids. Dad spends his life regretting making it a family business, despite commercial success.
- Dad can't decide what to do, so he splits the business between his two sons and retires. There is no tie-breaking mechanism. One son runs the factory and does the heavy lifting; the other does some marketing, runs other competing businesses, doesn't work too hard, and gets in the way of the first son.

- Four adult siblings own a business, the youngest, the CEO, is in his early seventies with no succession plan. The business is not performing. Everyone wants their dividend, but no one wants to make the tough decisions. The bank is about to call their loan.

So, what do all these scenarios have in common?

Call it like it is. With family conflicts, families tend to have one of two penchants: (1) To not want to say "we have an issue to discuss" since it causes discomfort, and (2) To immediately get aggressive at the first sign of conflict to get the upper hand. Neither is effective. A better way is to approach the parties in a calm voice, identify and define the issue, and advise that it needs to be addressed. This is the first step to outlining a process to address the issue, separate from the solution. Sometimes, just agreeing to talk about the issue is the hard part. People usually know there is a problem, even if no one is talking about it.

Define the issues. It is important to separate the person from the issue and business interests from personal interests. I can be angry that you decided to spend an excessive amount of money on client entertainment, but that judgment doesn't make you a bad person. It may mean you have poor judgment, and your department has bad performance, which can be dealt with separately. But focus on the issue that causes the conflict, not the person. We have business interests and personal interests. Even in family businesses, they are not the same. If someone is using the business as their piggy bank or not managing their responsibilities, that is a business issue. But if they waste their own money, unrelated to the business, that may be a tragedy, but it is likely not a business issue.

This is an important step to help take the emotions out of the conflict. What issue are you trying to address and resolve?

Get perspective before engaging. The more difficult the issue, the more likely the participants need perspective before entering negotiations. Parties may be certain they are right, but that is only based on their facts. Miles' Law states, "Where you stand depends on where you sit." You likely have to change where someone is sitting (give them more facts/perspective/data) if you want to change their position on the issues. This is also a function of time, age, and how their judgment evolves.

When in doubt, get facilitation. Sometimes, you need a third party to intervene. Managing the dialogue is different from deciding. This is why our society has professional mediators, negotiators, and facilitators. There is an art to getting disputing parties to talk about the issues and get a resolution. That is different from taking sides, picking a winner, or telling people what to do. Facilitators may be consultants, coaches, mediators, social workers, psychologists, or psychiatrists. When in doubt, get help.

Case Study: Deadlocked Cousins

In a recent assignment, I was asked to help a family business move forward. Two brothers started a business and achieved success. One brother had three children; his two sons took over the business when the dads retired. His daughter became a lawyer with no interaction with or ownership of the business. The second brother had a son (the attorney) and a daughter (the doctor), neither of who had a professional interest in the business. These two were passive outside owners who actively watched their investments.

Since they were brothers, the fathers did not need a tie-breaking mechanism in their operating agreement. But the children were trapped since the insiders and outsiders had different objectives and no mechanism to overcome the constant split deadlocks.

The two outsiders looked at the business as a financial investment. The two insiders were focused on their lifestyle and preserving the family legacy, but not driving growth and change in a tough business.

The cousins battled over numerous issues for years, causing the business to stagnate. The family cycled through several family business consultants who tried to work on the relationship issues. The last consultant suggested the family call me, which they did.

During the introductory session, I understood these were nice people; they didn't want to hurt each other, but they were not on the same page. Even within the sibling groups, there were different goals and objectives.

The board consisted of the two insiders, plus the attorney and the doctor, with no outsiders. I had to remind them that they each owed duties of care and loyalty to the other shareholders. If selling the business was the right decision, they had an obligation to do it, even if they were in the minority. They were so used to "thinking about me" that they had become ignorant of the basic rules of governance.

Then I asked a few simple questions:

- From a personal perspective:
    - How do you define success?
    - How much risk are you comfortable with at this point in life?
- From a business perspective:
    - How do you define success?
    - How much risk are you comfortable with?

They had become so wrapped up in their conflicts that they never stopped to think about what they were trying to get done. Some didn't know what they wanted because they were so frustrated, they never stopped to think about their priorities.

As a result of this, they engaged me to help them work through the issues to try to resolve their conflicts.

I spent a few hours with each person, working through these questions, forcing each individual to think about what they wanted and where they would compromise. As a result of the interviews, I knew where there was room to give and had confidence an agreement could be made.

I then consolidated the results and grouped the issues into three buckets:

- Issues where there are fundamental agreements, maybe needing a few tweaks
- Issues to be negotiated but should be resolvable with compromise
- Dealbreakers, topics that were black and white, and if they could not be addressed, the deadlock would remain

I have used this process in several other mediation processes, both family and non-family, and have found it to work well. The question is, "Is there a deal to be made?" not so much what the deal is. Unfortunately, not every situation has a happy ending. The goal of the process is to find out if a happy ending is possible.

Your Ownership Journey

Secret #8. Ownership Strategy Comes First

» Conflict can be healthy or unhealthy, but either way, it needs to be dealt with.

» Identifying and managing conflict is a necessary evil for any business owner, and many tools exist to assist with that process.

» Personal agendas can sometimes be negotiated.

» Personal values typically cannot be negotiated, except under a few extreme circumstances.

» Dismissing conflict in a family enterprise as greed is too easy. More likely, stakeholders are fighting about real emotional needs, such as self-purpose and personal identity.

» When the family bond does not provide enough leverage to achieve compromise or a commitment to personal change, litigation or separation might be the likely outcome.

Keep Getting Results

Author James N. Watkins famously said, "A river cuts through rock, not because of its power, but because of its persistence."

What does persistence mean for the ownership journey? After you have your ownership and business strategies in place, sufficient capital and the right talent, organic growth and/or growth by acquisition, proper governance, a plan for management success, and knowledge of how to defuse conflicts, what's next? That's simple: stay the course while adapting to changes along the way.

President Calvin Coolidge, who said, "The business of America is business," had this to say about staying the course:

> *Nothing in this world can take the place of persistence. Talent will not: nothing is more common than unsuccessful men with talent. Genius will not; unrewarded genius is almost a proverb. Education will not: the world is full of educated derelicts. Persistence and determination alone are omnipotent.*

Newspapers and magazines do a great job of informing us of others' success. Everyone loves a winner. I mentioned this earlier in the book, but the often-heard sentiment, "Success has a thousand fathers and failure is an orphan," bears repeating. There are several variations of this theme.

It is more fun to win. So, what are the unique characteristics that separate the winners from the also-rans, from the outright losers? Who wins is often as much of a test of character than much else. What characteristics always show up when you look at great business success across industries, decades, and centuries?

Innovation and disruption are the biggest creators of opportunity. The robber barons (first railroads in USA—Astor, Morgan, Fisk, Stanford), oil barons (first oil production in USA—Rockefeller, Hunt, Getty, Lucas), and software moguls (Gates, Ellison, Bezos, Zuckerberg) became billionaires because they were in the right place at the right time and had the skills and foresight to see that the world was changing. They also were able to, and chose to, take risks. For some of them, they likely lied, cheated, and stole as well.

Someone was going to invent the personal computer. IBM launched its PC in 1981. Ken Olsen built one of the first significant computer companies in the world, Digital Equipment Corporation. Founded in 1957, DEC was the industry leader for the first generation of distributed computing. Olsen famously said, "Why would anyone need a personal computer?" But Steve Jobs and Steve Wozniak figured out how to make and market it to best fit consumer needs. DEC failed to adapt to the market needs, and in 1998 was sold to Compaq. At that time, Compaq was the leading PC maker in the country.

There is a benefit to being in the right place at the right time and being blessed with the skills, intelligence, and connections to enter this pantheon of business greatness.

But hope is not a plan, and as an owner, you need a plan.

The robber barons, oil barons, and software moguls of the past were in the right place at the right time and blessed to have what was needed to take advantage of their once-in-a-century opportunities. But that is not what happens to everyone else. The rest of us need to soldier on, playing the cards we were dealt as best as possible.

So, what are the other characteristics that define successful owners of private companies? After analyzing dozens of case studies, these strategies come to mind:

Maintain Focus. Many entrepreneurs are known for being hyperactive and are typically accused of having ADHD or a similar condition. A high energy level is important to get results, but without focus, it is meaningless. You can run in circles super fast and still get nowhere.

Have Tenacity. President Coolidge was right about persistence and determination. But you can get tired if that is all you have to work with. It is not enough to work hard; you have to work on the right issues at the right time and bring in help when hard work alone is not going to get the job done.

Practice Adaptability. Charles Darwin is often misquoted as saying, "Survival of the fittest" when he meant, "Survival of the most adaptable." If you study his work, it makes sense. The same is true of businesses that endure over decades and centuries versus those that shine brightly for a few years and then burn out like a star. DEC is an example of a company that failed to adapt after forty years of success. Great companies can fail with new products that they bet their future on. Examples include Google Glass, Apple Newton, and New Coke.

Set Priorities. Business is not a democracy and should not be handing out participation trophies. Priorities matter because time, talent, and resources are scarce and must be allocated to their highest and best use. That is what owners need to focus on. If you don't get the priorities right, you are likely to get the wrong things done.

Manage Expectations. When you combine focus, adaptability, priorities, and a practical understanding of what your organization can do, it is time to manage expectations. This is both for yourself as an owner and for your management and staff. Two phrases that sum this up are stretch goals (set your goals just beyond your known reach, but not so far that they are unreasonable) and SMART goals, which are specific, measurable, achievable, relevant, and time-bound.

Ask For Help. Don't be afraid to ask for help when you need it. The Temptations said it well in 1966: "Ain't too proud to beg." It is important to maintain a healthy, balanced perspective of your situation. This can be tough when you are firefighting, perhaps lacking resources, or having a tough go of it. Even the best athletes have coaches, as do many executives. Sometimes a few pointers are all you need for a course correction. Other times you need someone to tell you what none of your people will say. Whether it is a coach, a personal board of directors, an advisory board, or a fiduciary board, you should be thinking of your current and future needs and surround yourself with people who can keep your thinking fresh and your eyes clear and provide clarity of judgment for when you may become conflicted.

Hold Yourself Accountable. This is often the hardest task of all. Few people do this well, consistently, year in and year out for decades. Several of the boards that I serve on were formed because the owners knew they needed outsiders to enforce accountability. This is a higher standard than "let's make some money and have some fun." This is the owner-ship version of the concept of continuous improvement.

Here are a few real-world examples where these key characteristics made the difference between success and something else.

Learning From The FurnCo Story

FurnCo[17] is a second-generation family business started in the 1980s. Dad worked for a business that imported products from Asia for domestic companies. One year, there was a disruption in the supply chain, and a customer asked: "Your service is so good; we can't get what we need. Can you find it for us?" And he did. Dad started importing products directly from Asian factories for his US clients. Then they started selling inexpensive electronic products under their name. The business grew to about $10 million in revenue, but sales were choppy since the product lifecycle was short and consumer tastes were fickle.

In 2008, the children, now running the company, received a painful reality check, as they almost went broke due to the financial crisis. They realized they needed a more reliable revenue stream, which meant different products and different customers. So, they adapted to the situation and completely remade the company. They formed a board of advisors to hold themselves accountable. They hired a strategy consultant to prioritize growth initiatives and create accountability throughout the organization. They managed expectations by setting annual SMART goals, and through tenacity, always met or exceeded their goals.

Ten years later, the company is completely different, and successful beyond their dreams. They have created globally best-in-class products and systems. Most importantly, they are having fun as they are close to arriving at their ownership goals.

Here is their score:

- Focus: Realized they needed to focus on steady cash flow to survive and be less seasonal
- Tenacity: Kept evolving their business model until they figured out what the market wanted
- Adaptability: Worked through dozens of product categories to find where they had a clear competitive advantage due to their sourcing, freight, and e-commerce knowledge
- Priorities: Put growth and cash flow first
- Expectations: Stayed humble despite increasing success

- Help: Hired several consultants to serve their ever-changing needs
- Accountability: Formed a board of advisors to hold themselves accountable

Lessons From The RealCo Story

RealCo is a real estate brokerage business. As a result of the 2008 crash, two entrepreneurial real estate investors found themselves out of work and a bit anxious. One had an idea about getting into the residential brokerage business since so many were failing at the time. They knew how to sell and how to run a business. So, they scrambled and bought a brokerage at a deep discount and learned the business. Then they found another one and another. Over ten years, they built one of the largest brokerages in the country. They adapted by starting other businesses that could sell highly profitable products to the same customers. They bought into the EOS process to systematize how they managed the business. Their culture was laser-focused on customer needs. They listened to their people. They constantly spoke to outsiders to get perspective, stay fresh, and learn. And they persevered every day. While I cannot share their details, they have been successful on every metric measured in business.

Here is their score:

- Focus: Need to feed their families and stay laser-focused on developing a winning plan
- Tenacity: Completed fifty small transactions over ten years to build an industry juggernaut

- Adaptability: Had to structure each deal differently to get it done but figured out how to make it work to achieve a higher goal
- Priorities: Put growth and cash flow first
- Expectations: Never changed how they worked together or their culture, despite success
- Help: Adopted EOS to run the business, and the CEO joined YPO to help him look ahead
- Accountability: Measured themselves against a long-term plan and were honest with themselves about their achievements

Understanding The Success And Failure Of TradeCo

The third case is TradeCo, one of the early high-frequency trading firms in the financial markets. A group of floor traders at the CBOT had the idea in 2001 that computers could be used to trade futures and options. They used their profits from floor trading to write code. They could see where things were going, even though no one had done it before. So, they started writing code, developing infrastructure, signing data agreements, and hunting for a new type of talent, not in their industry.

They knew the issue was speed; whoever was fastest would win the trade and keep the profit. They started to swap out servers every few months just to get the slightest edge. They plowed their floor-trading profits into building the software infrastructure needed to dominate their markets. Unlike Furnco and RealCo, they had outsized expectations. But since their industry was being reinvented, they assessed that the unrealistic was, in fact, realistic.

In a few years, the business grew from $1.6 million to over $100 million in revenue, and TradeCo became one of the defining forces in the industry until there was a change in leadership.

Two of the four founders saw that the industry was changing, yet again, and this time it was not for the better. The two remaining owners bought them out. The remaining two started to enjoy the spoils more than focus on the future. The next generation of leaders stepped up, cut from a different cloth.

Three years later, the business was sold to pay for the buyouts of the two exiting founders. Profits fell off precipitously, and the leadership did not recognize, accept, and adapt to the new reality.

They went from rags to riches to rags in less than ten years.

Here is their score:

- Focus: While they focused on building a great trading company, they did well. When they lost focus, they lost their business.
- Tenacity: As you can see from the other examples, focus and tenacity tend to go together. When TradeCo lost its focus, it also lost its tenacity.
- Adaptability: In the early years, the company constantly shifted its technical architecture and infrastructure to meet a rapidly evolving marketplace. When they stopped adapting, it became the beginning of their end.

- Priorities: TradeCo was successful while it had a clear and simple set of priorities. When their priorities drifted to things outside the workplace, profits dissipated.
- Expectations: In fact, their outsized expectations were justified in the early days since the opportunity was there, and everything else aligned. But the market moved, they missed it, and because of this, they failed to reset expectations for themselves and their staff.
- Help: In the early days, the leadership was quick to help with a broad set of business issues. But when they got into trouble, they wouldn't listen to anyone.
- Accountability: The need for accountability doesn't waver depending on this year's results. You either hold yourself accountable, or you don't. They didn't hold themselves accountable, and they lost their business because of it.

Management Systems

Being an owner or CEO is often considered one of the loneliest jobs, and for a good reason. Over time, leaders have developed peer groups to help each other and management systems for running their businesses.

For private companies, some of the better-known leadership groups are EOS, Vistage, and YPO. While these are the bigger brand names, there are numerous others and several variations of all the above.

I recommend that, from time to time, you assess your needs and explore if something like this helps you achieve your vision. If so, then join. If not, find what works best for you instead. Consider these:

EOS. The Entrepreneurship Operating System is a system of tools and practices to help entrepreneurs run their businesses. It has worked for many of my clients but is not for every business. I see that you have to be "all in" for it to work; if you cherry-pick things that you like, it doesn't have the desired impact.

Vistage. Formerly known as TEC, Vistage International is a peer mentoring group that caters to owners, CEOs, and other executives. Members are organized in groups of ten to twelve who are not competitors, and a chair runs their meetings. Most Vistage members become members for life, and the brotherly bonds formed extend to other parts of their lives.

YPO. The Young Presidents Organization is for CEOs appointed before the age of forty-five and serves businesses of some minimum size.

My observation is that, and these are not rules, smaller companies gravitate to EOS since it provides the structure they need at that stage of development. Vistage members tend to have businesses in the $10 million to $100 million revenue range, and YPO attracts CEOs of larger companies.

There are many ways to grow a successful business. The same business can use different systems under different leadership at different times and stages of development.

There are as many exceptions as there are points of view. What is important is that you assess your needs at each stage of your ownership journey and get the help and advice to help you move forward toward your ownership goals.

How To Improve Your Business Resilience

If you are running a business today, you have likely lived through the October 1987 crash, 9/11, the 2008 recession, and now a global pandemic. Black swan events are a part of life, just not everyday occurrences. You should expect challenges, and they call for resilience.

Business resilience is a concept with a new meaning in the post-COVID-19 world. It has been defined by the National Association of Corporate Directors (NACD) as "the capacity of any entity to prepare for disruptions, to recover from shocks and stresses, and then to adapt and grow from a disruptive experience." Resilience is the demonstrated ability to move forward—better.

Numerous technical standards give their definitions of resilience, such as ISO 22316:2017, which describes resilience as an ability, and more specifically, the capacity to absorb and adapt in a non-static environment to deliver its objectives while surviving and thriving.

Within the world of technology, ITIL4 also recognizes resilience as an ability. It occurs when an organization can predict, prepare for, react to, and adapt to minute changes and sudden impacts from external sources. Like NACD, ITIL4 acknowledges resilience as the ability to take a hit, get back up, and move forward.

Disaster recovery plans are associated with security breaches, fires, and hurricanes. But resilience is about survival and adaptation. If you take a moment to ponder the difference between fitness versus adaptability, it should be clear that they are not the same concepts.

When you comb through the numerous definitions and examples of business resilience, what stands out is that it is about how a group of people deals with adversity, communicates on priorities and risks, and makes decisions to move forward, all despite a lack of information, amid great uncertainty and likely in great peril.

Resilience is an absolute measure of the management team's ability to manage change and uncertainty. There is a reason people say, "It's all about the people." Leadership needs to manage the team in the moment, much as a captain steers a ship through a storm.

To be better prepared for the next event, ask yourself these three questions:

What did your team do better than expected during these stress periods?

You should get input from your team on this one and then synthesize what the numerous examples point out. Did a few heroes solve the big problems, or did everyone pull together?

Critically, listen to what people are not saying. That is usually the most important takeaway from this type of exercise. For example, you may hear, "Wow, the leadership stepped up and showed us the way forward. We could not have done it without them," or "We were scared about what was going to happen but working with our management made a bad situation much easier to deal with." If you do not hear this, why not?

Where were you blindsided when you should have been prepared?

If so, do you understand why? Was it due to systemic issues or unrelated causes? Were they foreseeable at all? What flaw in your risk management system caused these issues to be surprises, and what part of the system is so broken that it allowed this to happen? If the cause of the issue is within the boardroom and not the management team, how is the board getting feedback and being held accountable to protect ownership?

What aspects of your culture and governance need to improve so you have greater resilience in the future?

Everyone knows culture is the straw that stirs the business' drink, but there are no obvious levers to pull to make changes. Especially with culture, change must come from the top of the organization. The old saw is that "children watch what you do, not what you say," which is also true in a business setting.

Introspection and the ability to challenge yourself with intellectual honesty are the hallmarks of critical thinking. They require discipline and are likely to be uncomfortable, but they need to be done.

Waste A Serious Crisis

Board members are tasked with evaluating how their businesses handle difficult periods, such as: How did we do? What could we have done better? How do we prepare for the next crisis?

This process demands that boards grapple with great complexity methodically. The goal is to assess performance to determine what capabilities are lacking, then build those capabilities in advance of the next crisis. Businesses that pull through crises do so because leadership has cultivated the ability to expect the unexpected.

As Rahm Emanuel reminded us back in 2008, "You never want a serious crisis to go to waste." Here are several essential strategies boards can employ to survive crises similar to the COVID-19 crisis and capitalize on the experience.

Assess The Situation

Perspective is a function of time. We've hit the first bench-mark, where we have enough perspective to engineer our approach to the future. This doesn't mean that you won't get things wrong or that your perspective won't change. But it's important to take stock of the situation today.

Ask yourself: Did our risk management system work? If we did not have a risk management system, what did that cost us? How would we rate our response? How well were we able to communicate with our employees, customers, and suppliers? Did we have enough liquidity to survive the crisis? Being brutally honest about your performance is difficult, but it is the best way to evolve your governance processes.

Analyze Consumer Behavior

Businesses need a clear understanding of how consumer patterns shifted during the pandemic and which shifts are short-term versus long-term. Did your customers stop buying luxury items in favor of essentials? Did they switch to a different price point or delay spending?

Did you experience an uplift that correlated with government stimulus? According to the US Census Bureau, 80 percent of American households spent stimulus money on food, half bought household and personal care products, and about 8 percent purchased goods like electronics and fitness equipment. If you did see a huge uplift with government stimulus, understand that probably won't happen again.

Determining exactly what your customers did differently during the crisis will inform how you adjust your business and communicate those changes to your employees, customers, and suppliers.

Adjust Your Marketing

This might have meant bigger marketing spend next year, especially if your supply chain took a hit. If, for example, the aluminum shortage prevented you from packaging and shipping your product, you might have spent the bulk of next year telling your customers why they should still love you.

Your customers will not care about issues with your supply chain; they will care about how you handle those issues. It still holds true that if you're making excuses, you're probably not winning. Even if your business isn't responsible for its problems, your customers will still hold you accountable.

Adapt Your Approach

COVID-19 picked winners and losers by industry. You must understand your fate and adapt to it. If you're in the travel and hospitality industry, you may question your ability to survive. If you're in the grocery store business, your outlook is probably pretty good. Your path forward will vary dramatically by your industry and the size of your business. Even though the pandemic has impacted us all, there is no one-size-fits-all solution.

Plan Your Next Budget Cycle

October is when most businesses plan the following year's budget cycle. This process usually begins by asking, "How did we do last year?" and then making the necessary adjustments. But what if that year was not typical, such as 2020, which was far from a typical year? In that case, boards might have needed to go back to 2019 and see which assumptions still held and apply the lessons they learned in 2020 to plan for 2021 and beyond.

Evaluate Management's Character

This is an important time for boards to evaluate the character of their management teams. How did they handle the immediate crisis? Did they panic? Do your employees admire them for their efforts? How has management's response impacted the business' reputation?

Crises build great management teams. When things are going well, everyone looks good. But when the tide goes out, you can easily see who isn't wearing shorts. Boards are tasked with evaluating management's performance. If it was poor, did they learn valuable lessons? Were they valiant in their efforts to do the right thing, or did they cut and run?

If management failed, despite making the best possible decisions with the available information, it might be that no one could have won in that situation. In this case, success stems from strong character and its impact on your employees' motivation.

Motivation might be your business' best asset right now. When things are bad, employees will follow leaders who demonstrate strong character. Ultimately, this kind of leadership is what separates good companies from great companies. Character can be the difference between which companies survive and which don't.

Summing Up

Simple resilience is about bouncing back to the status quo, going back to how things were before the crisis hit. Complex resilience is when we learn, grow, and adapt, finding new skills and perspectives, which help us to be prepared for the next crisis.[18]

The characteristics that get results do not depend on your industry, size, or stage of development. They are the gravitational forces of success. You need to evaluate yourself constantly to see if you are doing what is needed to achieve your goals.

Everyone dies or retires, but you only get to pick one. If you want to be assured of successfully retiring, you need to have a plan that gets you there. One fine day you may need to sell your business. Understanding how a business sale works is the topic of the following chapter.

Your Ownership Journey

Secret #9. Keep Getting Results

» When things are bad, employees will follow leaders who demonstrate strong character. Ultimately, this kind of leadership is what separates great companies from good companies.

» Businesses that pull through crises do so because leadership has cultivated the ability to expect the unexpected.

» Resilience is an absolute measure of the management team's ability to manage change. There is a reason people say that "it's all about the people."

» If you are running a business today, you have likely lived through the October 1987 crash, 9/11, the 2008 recession, and now a global pandemic. Black swan events are a part of life, just not everyday occurrences. You should expect them.

» Disaster recovery plans are associated with security breaches, fires, hurricanes, and other singular events. Business resilience is about survival and adaptation to existential problems.

Know How Selling A Business Works

Mark Cuban got it wrong, in my opinion.

Cuban, the owner of the NBA's Dallas Mavericks and star of the TV show *Shark Tank*, said: "Don't start a company unless you have an obsession and something you love. If you have an exit strategy, it's not an obsession."

Yes, you need to be obsessed with your business to achieve success. But everyone has an exit plan: they will either die or retire. Diet, exercise, and sleep are how to plan for the former, but business exit planning is how to deal with the latter.

My view is that even the obsessed owners who love their business need to have an exit strategy. They need to know how selling a business works. The adage, "We'll cross that bridge when we come to it," isn't always the right answer.

One of my consistent experiences is seeing that most people don't buy and sell companies, so when it's time for them to sell their own business, it's the first such transaction of their life—and the most important thing they're ever going to do. However, they are often like babes in the woods, with everyone else knowing what the game's rules are except them.

As a business owner, you need to realize that if you know nothing about the rules of the game to sell a business, you need help. And from what I have seen, most owners are wholly unprepared to make this extremely important decision, and it's sure not one they want to screw up. As they say in poker, "If you don't know who the fool at the table is, it's you."

The Roadmap To Selling Your Business

While most business owners may have mastered the art of starting and operating a business, few are familiar with the necessary steps to successfully sell that business. I have guided many business owners through the pre-sales process with the aim of ensuring they are adequately rewarded for all the economic and sweat equity they put into the business upon their exit.

One of the first things you must do when preparing for a business sale is to understand your industry dynamics. That means analyzing the following aspects of your industry:

What is controllable versus non-controllable? You are responsible for what you can control and are expected to adapt to that which you cannot control.

Growth rate and profitability. The industry determines your growth rate and profitability, typically within a narrow range. The only way to break out of the range is to innovate or disrupt the industry. That is why certain tech and healthcare firms receive high valuations compared to their peers. Fracking is another example.

Externalities/regulation. If you are in a highly regulated industry, such as financial services or healthcare, the regulations control the industry. But they are not market forces; they are the result of negotiations between the industry, consumers, and the governmental bodies that regulate the industry.

Rate of change: If your industry is undergoing rapid change (remember Michael Porter's model), then your future may be up in the air. You need to have some vision of the future of your industry to assess your options.

With that information in hand, you need to set realistic expectations for the sale, which starts by determining the answers to the following questions:

What is the true value of your business? Your business is only worth what a willing buyer will pay. Most sellers start with unrealistic expectations and become frustrated with what they see as low bids. In the end, the market is always right; it is just waiting for you to adjust to what you may not want to accept.

What do you want to get from a sale versus what you need to get to be able to retire? This is often the biggest issue for sellers, especially if they have not been saving for retirement through their working lives. The sell decision should start with a thorough discussion with your financial advisors to assure your future financial security with a reasonable margin of safety.

What is the best time to transition? This decision will be at the confluence of several forces: the business; your health, energy, and interests; and your financial planning. Each of these needs to be understood before starting the sale process.

How should you deal with partners and/or family owners? Stakeholders are just as important to consider, even if they do not have a vote. This is about how you want to handle the important relationships in your life, as well as the people who are critical to your business success. Thoughts of legacy come into play here.

How can you prevent seller's remorse? Too many people have sold their business and spent the rest of their lives regretting the outcome. The regret is typically not financial, but how important relationships soured due to events or what future owners did with the business. A big pile of money does not make this any easier. The smartest owners focus on this point.

Walk-Away Number Calculation

If you're like many business owners, your business is your retirement plan, so what you will walk away with is a critical number. The best way to illustrate this is with two calculations: your walk-away number and your magic number. The former is the net proceeds you would receive from a sale after taxes and expenses. The latter is the minimum net proceeds you need to comfortably secure your lifestyle for the rest of your life, in addition to other specific financial goals (e.g., paying for grandchildren's college) that are important to you.

For the purposes of this example, let's say the owner bought the business for $5 million; the transaction value is $30 million and the capital gains tax rate is 25 percent; the banker fee is 4 percent; and the lawyer, consultant, and accountant fees are $150,000.

So, the walk-away number is:

Walk-away Calculation

Transaction value	$30,000,00
Cost Basis	$5,000,000
Gain	**$25,000,000**
Capital gains tax	($6,250,000)
Banker fee	($1,200,000)
Lawyer and other fees	($150,000)
Walk-away Number	**$17,400,000**

As a rule of thumb, with federal and state capital gains tax at 25 percent, the net proceeds are typically 70 percent of the gain.

Magic Number Calculation

The sale of the business hopefully provides ample retirement funds. This calculation is based on the 3 percent rule, which is the concept that in a well-diversified, professionally managed investment portfolio, you can withdraw about 3 percent per year without materially diminishing the corpus over time. This concept does have certain assumptions that your financial advisor can provide. For instance, let's assume nominal inflation.

In the example above, this owner should draw about $522,000 per year in net proceeds indefinitely if the assumptions hold true. Talk to your financial advisor about running Monte Carlo simulations to see how this may work for you.

A Typical Timeline

Part of considering an exit is to think about the timing. This is a process, not an event, and multiple workstreams need to be coordinated.

Your timeline considerations will include:

- Health and personal energy at each stage
- Financial position for the present and future
- Second career options and endeavors
- Opportunity set for the present and future

Selling a business takes time and happens in two phases. The first phase is used to prepare the business and for the owners to go to market. The second phase is the actual sale process.

Optimizing Valuation/ Preparing A Business For Sale

If you are serious about selling the business, then you need to get prepared for the process. Smart owners may begin their positioning as long as three to five years before they want to get out. You may need up to a year to transact.

If the business is well-run and nicely profitable, the books and records are up to par, and there is a complete management team with adequate succession plans, there may not be much to prepare.

But if the books and records are sloppy, the management team is thin, performance has been lacking, and the customer base is challenged, it will take more time. If you fix these issues before selling the company, you get paid for it. If you don't, then the buyer must fix them and will discount the price accordingly.

Here are four areas to focus on as you prepare for your business for sale:

Business changes

- Do you have specific KPIs and metrics for each facet of your business?
- Do you have a culture of accountability, or do you need to make improvements?
- What do you need to do now operationally to prepare?
- What operational changes should occur post-sale?

Internal organization

- Form an internal deal team
- Develop a communications plan for employees, customers, suppliers, and your local communities

Finance and IT

- Upgrade the financial team to be on par with the buyers
- Confirm that the trailing thirty-six months of financial statements are properly stated
- Conduct a thorough IT/cyber assessment and prepare an action plan to resolve inadequacies

Get the right people for the challenge ahead

- Evaluate bankers, lawyers, accountants, and specialists
- Consider the deals they have done that are most similar to yours
- Give yourself enough time to decide who is the best fit for your team

Your Fiduciary Duty

As you weigh your options, there are several questions to ask yourself, revolving around the biggest question: What would a prudent person do in this situation? Unless you own 100 percent of the business, you will have a fiduciary duty to protect minority owners. Is the transaction going to be fair to all shareholders? Does it meet their liquidity needs? Does it provide growth capital for the business if that is a goal? What flexibility does it provide for future liquidity and growth capital needs? Is it efficient for tax and estate planning purposes?

Having worked with many owners who have made this transition, I cannot stress enough how important it is to start the tax and estate planning work early. These are not decisions to be made in a rush, and it is often difficult to fully contemplate the consequences of each decision. Building a thoughtful decision tree takes time.

Since you are making decisions that are likely to alter the life of your children and grandchildren, you need to get good advice. To help you to understand these issues, see the advice of Lauren Wolven in Secret #12.

Key Stages Of The Deal

Since this is likely the most significant transaction of your life, it is important to know the key stages of the deal:

Preparing to go to market. The first four to eight weeks of the process are used to prepare the documents that will define the process. There is typically a confidential information memorandum (CIM), a fifty- to eighty-page PowerPoint deck describing the business in detail. A subset of the CIM is the teaser, a one- to two-page document excluding confidential information used to alert buyers of the opportunity and solicit interest. The CIM is written first, and the teaser is extracted from it. Buyers excited by the teaser will sign a non-disclosure agreement (NDA) before receiving the CIM.

In parallel to writing the CIM, the bankers will develop a buyers list for the seller to approve. This could be as many as three hundred firms that the bankers think will want to know about the deal. The sellers review the list to exclude parties they know they won't sell to or where the risks of providing the CIM are too great, despite legal protections.

Sellers are often advised to prepare a quality of earnings report (QoE) as part of the preparation process. This is a highly detailed financial analysis of the income statement, balance sheet, and cash flows, which normalize reporting to how buyers view the business.

For example, if an owner has their grade-school kids on the payroll or expenses their vacations to the business, those expenses would be added back to profits since the buyer will not have those expenses. The QoE process normally pays for itself several times over. However, some buyers will take that report and hire financial experts to review it for credibility.

Indications of interest. After buyers have signed the NDA, reviewed the CIM, and had several conversations with the banker, they will submit non-binding indications of interest. This short letter states how they value the business (a range), the structure of the deal, how they will pay for it, and what they intend to do with the business. It will likely state the assumptions upon which these decisions are made. That means if the assumptions change during diligence, so does the price. When the indications of interest are in hand, the seller chooses which buyers move forward in the process. While price is a key driver, deal structure, management issues, and legacy concerns are considered.

Management presentations and diligence. The next major hurdle is the management presentations (MPs). These tend to be three- to four-hour meetings where the sellers present the company to the buyers. The purpose of the MPs is to help the buyers understand the opportunity and for management to showcase its abilities. The bankers typically recraft the CIM as a spoken presentation, highlighting key investment theses and working around concerns that may reduce value and the ability to close. Sellers need to practice the MPs several times to get it right, often highlighting each team member's expertise and industry knowledge. In parallel with the MPs, the buyers will perform detailed market and financial diligence to better understand the business.

Binding letters of intent. A few weeks after the MPs, the buyers will be asked to submit final binding letters of intent (LoIs). These will look like indications of interest but with more detail. They are the framework for the legal documents that will edify the transaction. Once the LoIs are submitted, there are likely to be several phone calls to clarify the details and calibrate the nuances.

Selecting a buyer. At this point, the seller selects one buyer to transact with and agrees not to talk to any other buyers for sixty to ninety days. Buyers will spend considerable resources to get to the closing table and want to make sure the seller is committed to the deal. This does not mean the deal is guaranteed to get done, but the seller will not use the primary buyer as a stalking horse to get a better deal elsewhere.

Diligence and documentation. From here until the closing, it is a multi-track sprint. Financial, legal, HR, regulatory, market, and operational diligence go full tilt. The lawyers start to draft documents and negotiate terms. Executives start to negotiate their new employment agreements.

The LoI captures the major business terms, but as the lawyers start drafting, they will identify details the LoI did not address. There will be a steady back-and-forth between buyer and seller and their respective attorneys as these details get resolved. This part of the process can be exhausting. Selling a business is like running a marathon and then making an uphill sprint.

Closing and transition. Once there is agreement on all the business and legal items, a closing is scheduled. While you may have worked hard for nine months to get there, the sign of a successful closing is that it is uneventful. You sign numerous documents, wait around for the lawyers to do their thing, and then they tell you it is done. You check your bank account to see a big number. Don't forget to execute your communication plan to employees, customers, and other stakeholders to get the right message. If you agree to an earn-out, you have more work to do.

During the final stages, a transition plan is constructed, including when and how the deal will be announced, staffing changes, and other operational details.

You are now in the next stage of life.

Types Of Buyers

As you move through the selling process, remember the two types of buyers: financial and strategic. Even though their goals may differ, high-quality buyers exist in both universes, but you should be aware of their pros and cons.

Financial Buyers

- Must return capital and profits to investors
- Must earn competitive returns to survive
- Driven by fund structure
- Dependent on debt markets to compete
- Buy platforms, and then add-on deals occur
- Must put money to work
- Fees are usually a 2 percent and 20 percent structure

Strategic Buyers

- Deals are tied to the CEO's vision
- Tend to be large or public companies
- Looking for brands, product lines, technology, or certain assets
- Require strong synergies to drive needs
- Usually, a source of permanent capital
- Don't have to put money to work

Integration Issues

Before deciding to agree for your business to be acquired by another entity, you must answer a few internal evaluation questions:

- How will the two different cultures be integrated?
- What will be done with the management team?
- How will customers view this?
- How does this drive revenue?
- Where will costs be cut?
- How will business systems be consolidated?

What To Remember

As you move through the transaction process, never lose sight of the following three things:

- Stay disciplined and focused on the process.
- Adjust to what the market is saying because the market is always right.
- Play the game as a team sport.

How To Sell A Private Business For The Best Value

For most business owners, selling a business is a once-in-a-lifetime event. These owners want to maximize their proceeds, and they may be super salespeople but likely have little experience or don't know how to sell a small business. Their exit may be the only meaningful transaction they experience. Therefore, the business owner needs to choose between using an intermediary, such as an investment banker or a business broker, or managing the process themself.

Owners talk to other owners and share experiences, and sometimes war stories abound. These can lead to hesitation on the owner's part. But, at some point, every ownership group must transition out.

During a recent board session on exit planning, the owner announced it was time to sell, and the board supported this conclusion. The business had been profitable for twenty years, and the owner was ready to retire. The owner was thinking about running the sale himself, but the board cautioned him to consider how to get the most value for a lifetime of work. I was asked to summarize the client's options on moving forward, knowing that the size of the deal could determine that choice.

There are three choices to explore when it's time to sell your company:

Hire an investment banker. If you don't know how to sell a business, consider an investment banker the most qualified to run the sale process. They typically have the deepest resources and the best information on deal structure and valuations. However, their minimum fees run from $500,000 to $1 million (depending on the circumstance). For a business under $1 million to $2 million EBITDA, this is usually not an option.

Once you sign an engagement letter, there will be a whirlwind of activity. The process is likely to run for six to nine months. Bankers deliver value throughout the sale process: According to JD Merit, an investment banker can increase the sale price by 5 to 20 percent on average.[19] Bankers specialize by industry. It is important to know the dominant players within the industry. Consider the personal chemistry of who you may work with. You will be spending a lot of time with the banking team and have difficult discussions. Owners should pick a bank team that they can work well with during tough times.

Use a business broker. For businesses too small to be attractive to an investment bank, the downmarket version of this service is a business broker. While a broker provides a similar service, they typically do not have comparable resources. They are likely to lack the marketing horsepower, valuation databases, and market knowledge of an investment bank. Brokers and banks don't compete; instead, they serve different market niches. For many private firms, this may be the best or only option. Brokers serve a critical role in the lower middle market. They are different from banks because market forces require them. The relationship is more personal than with a bank. Typically, the brokerage consists of one or two brokers. Business brokers tend to be more pragmatic than a bank because their clients are not as complicated as the larger clients that a bank services. In general, business brokers can provide guidance with laws and regulations, save you time, and help maintain confidentiality during the sale process.

Sell your company yourself. There are skilled CEOs with great industry relationships, knowledge of the best buyers, and great negotiating skills. If that is the case, the marketing function of a bank or broker does not add value. With a good lawyer, it is certainly possible to get a fair deal done. And knowing how to sell a business is also a great way to avoid fees.

Other Issues To Consider

Regardless of which path you choose, consider a few issues:

Price. This is important, but the certainty of the close becomes precious as the process moves forward. Once you are invested in the process, you want to get it done as quickly as possible. While greed will dominate emotions during the bidding process, fear is prevalent as the risks of failure become more obvious.

Terms and conditions. Typically, terms and conditions determine long-term satisfaction with the transaction. People don't talk about the extra money they received if they are unhappy that they did not consider what potential conflicts could have been avoided.

As with most choices in business, getting the right team in place creates the foundation for success. This is true for running a going concern, as well as running a single transaction. Professionals can get you close to the finish line, but you will likely need to make the last push to success alone.

How To Not Have Regrets When Selling Your Business

Over time, I have seen that people who own and operate a business often view selling their company as a means to an end, whereas professionals handling transactions make their living doing deals. The former tend to look at transactions as an arrow in their strategy quiver, while the latter view buying and selling businesses as their business.

Many private and family business owners are never involved in such a transaction until they decide to sell their own business. The accepted practices, knowledge, and customs are foreign to them, making them both disadvantaged and distrusting during the process.

When working with owners who lack transaction experience, I start by sharing the lessons I learned from being in their position. Since selling my first company, I've made dozens of deals and have spoken to those who have been down this path as well, which have given me further perspective on the transaction process.

Below are a few lessons I've learned that can help you avoid any regrets when going through one of these transactions to sell your business.

Start With The Answer And Work Backward

If you have clear goals and objectives, it is easier to align the professionals helping you manage the process. Your goals are your compass, but in my experience, it is common for business owners to think about a transaction while struggling to articulate their goals. This means you need more education and decision support; you likely need help to understand the decisions and consequences before you.

To help with this, find out how willing the investment bank you're considering working with is to invest in owner education and handholding before signing an engagement letter. This is a bright-line test of fit between the parties.

If the bankers do their job right, there will be a clear set of goals before starting the process, and you will have a deep understanding of what to expect, both good and bad, when the dust settles. The issues include majority and minority control, ability to roll over capital, price expectations, financial security, time commitment after the transaction, marketability, and unique legacy issues.

The Market Is Always Right

"Managing seller expectations" is a common phrase that is a polite way of saying a business is often not worth what a seller expects. A business is only worth what a willing buyer will pay at a point in time. In deep and liquid markets, the final bid clears the market, meaning supply and demand are matched, and no buyers are willing to pay more.

But there are two issues here: value and timing. In one case, we had a binding term sheet to sell a business at an agreed price, with the closing scheduled for March 2020. Once COVID-19 hit, valuations changed due to new uncertainties not priced into the deal. With great effort, we were able to get the business sold in November 2020, at 67 percent of the prior price. While the value had changed, the terms had also changed. The bank financing became seller paper (which defers when the seller gets their cash), and the earn-out was a bigger part of the consideration. So the valuation was reduced, and much of the risk was shifted from the buyer back to the seller.

My advice to owners is to first listen to what the bankers are saying about valuation. Second, if you don't like the pricing, do something about it because it is still your business. Third, don't dawdle toward closing. Get it done while the facts are known because negative surprises can and do happen.

Another part of the ownership journey is to understand that (with apologies to Irving Berlin's Broadway musical, *Annie Get Your Gun*) there is no business like family business, like no business I know. That will be explored in the following chapter.

Your Ownership Journey

Secret #10. Know How Selling A Business Works

» As a business owner, you need to realize that if you know nothing about the rules of the game to sell a business, you need help.

» A business is only worth what a willing buyer will pay at a point in time.

» My advice to owners is to first listen to what the bankers are saying about valuation. If you don't like the pricing, do something about it because it is still your business.

» Price is important, but certainty of closing becomes precious as the process moves forward. Once you are invested in the exit process, you want to get it done as quickly as possible.

» Typically, terms and conditions determine long-term satisfaction with the transaction. People don't talk about the extra money they receive if they are unhappy with the outcome.

Understand How Family Businesses Are Different

In his book *Anna Karenina*, Leo Tolstoy wrote, "All happy families are all alike; each unhappy family is unhappy in its own way."

Known as the Anna Karenina principle, this applies to succession planning in family business and statistical significance tests, the failed domestication of animals, ecological risk assessments, and losing sports teams.

After studying numerous family business successes and failures, I've seen that successful transitions exhibit consistent traits. When studying failures, we see that they lack enough competence in many traits to achieve a critical mass of success factors.

The dynamics of a family business are quite different from those in place at a non-family business, so these enterprises deserve a chapter of their own.

The Highlights Of The Three Circle Model

Even after forty years, the Three Circle Model of Family Business is still an effective tool for dealing with the challenges of running a family business. The model was developed at Harvard Business School by Renato Tagiuri and John Davis in 1978.[20]

Governance maturity is measured by how evolved the critical structures are within each circle.

Three Circle Model

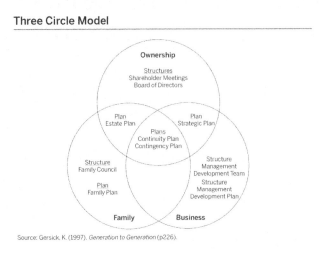

Source: Gersick, K. (1997). *Generation to Generation* (p226).

Family circle. The Family circle encompasses issues of the family, separate from their ownership and management duties. It includes the children and in-laws who do not have ownership and are not involved in the business. They may lack ownership, but they still have interests to consider. The family council and family assembly are the structures used to manage the Family circle issues.

Ownership circle. Shareholder meetings and boards of directors speak for ownership. The family needs to give direction to the business through the annual shareholder meeting and the board. The board is the critical bridge between the business and the individuals in the family.

Business circle. The Business circle includes the strategic plan, management succession, and contingency planning for the business. It is almost always the most evolved of the three circles.

The overlap between the Family and Ownership circles is the estate plans of the individual owners. The overlap between the Ownership and Business circles includes the strategic plans of the business. Finally, the overlap between the Business and Family circles is the continuity plans to assure the business' survival. The interconnectedness and evolving nature of each circle create layers of complexity to manage.

States Of Governance Maturity

Typically, the structures within the Business circle are the most evolved, ever-increasing as the business grows in size and complexity. The structures within the Family circle are typically the least evolved, since developing a family council and assembly touches on the most sensitive issues, including succession planning and estate planning. With small businesses, management succession plans and business continuity plans may also be lacking.

Many family businesses have an owner-centric board, whether a consultative, advisory, or true fiduciary board.

I have observed from forty years of working with family businesses that families with more mature governance processes tend to have a more informed, deliberative decision-making process and are more likely to make consensual decisions. A 2019 study from KPMG provides the data to confirm this observation.[21]

Family businesses have long been said to have two disadvantages compared to public companies: raising capital and attracting the best talent. But family businesses can fine-tune their governance processes to their precise needs. They should take advantage of the opportunity.

How To Assess The Governance Maturity Of A Family Business

To compare and balance the governance maturity of each structure, start by diagramming the three circles: Family, Ownership, and Business. Then ask yourself:

- Are the three circles well-defined or muddled?
- Is there accountability in each of the circles?
- Who makes decisions within each circle, and how do they do so?
- Is conflict identified, discussed, and managed? Or is it ignored?

The answers to these questions are co-dependent. If the circles are muddled, then there is likely unclear accountability. If accountability is lacking, then decision-making processes become more variable. If decision-making is variable, then conflict is more likely to arise.

You've Assessed The Three-Circle Model Of Family Business, Now What?

Basic problem-solving says start by defining what you do know and what can't be known. Diagram the situation and find out where decision-makers agree. From there, flush out the issues that need to be addressed. Tackle the easy issues first and take them off the table. Assess which issues are resolvable and go after them next. The issues most likely to be "deal breakers" should be held aside until there is a better framework for addressing them. They are likely to be emotionally charged matters.

Like a bowl of spaghetti, the issues are tangled. It takes time to work through them. But when you measure time in generations—not quarters—you realize there is always enough time to make changes if there is the desire and commitment to achieve change. This usually starts with education, helping the owners understand why they need to develop the governance structures today to protect the business and the family for future generations. One of the easiest ways to begin this process is using the Three-Circle Model of Family Business.

Eight Concepts To Help Plan And Manage Your Family Business

Here are the things that successful family businesses can do to stay a family business through generations:

The kids work somewhere else first. Preferably, they also earn a promotion before entering the family business. This is all for the kids' benefit. They will learn about the world, get a sense of who they are, come to understand the workplace, and start to mature while also assessing their skills and interests. Why not do that on someone else's dime? If they are going to have a failure, it is better to do it outside the family business. Then they have time to recover before entering the family business. Importantly, they need to make a voluntary decision to join the family business; they need to choose to leave something.

The kids start at the bottom and work their way up. It is difficult to succeed if you don't understand the details of the business. Few people become successful CEOs without understanding all facets of the enterprise. Without sufficient preparation, they are poorly equipped to lead.

If possible, the child works for an uncle or aunt rather than the parent. While this is not an option for most family businesses, consider having the child work for an executive outside the immediate family who has the personality to manage that child. The child needs a tutor, mentor, and boss who is not influenced by the parent-child relationship. Even if this is only for a few years, it helps the child build a strong professional foundation.

Every family chooses either business first or family first. One is not better than the other, but you need to be honest about the choice and develop family governance based on this choice. It is going to happen de facto if not de jure. If family comes first, business performance may suffer from its best potential, but that may be the price of family harmony. If business comes first, family relationships are likely not to be as close, and there is a greater likelihood of selling the business sooner.

Employment and ownership are different. Working in the business and having ownership in the business are two different constructs. Effective family governance will establish guidelines for employment and compensation separate from the benefits of ownership.

Economics and control should be separated to reduce conflicts. The two elements of ownership are economics and control. Successful family businesses often have two classes of stock: voting and nonvoting. When parents consider their estate plan, they may want to make money equal. Sometimes this means directing voting stock to the kids working in the business and nonvoting stock to the non-working children.

Fair does not mean equal. Doing what is fair does not always mean treating everyone equally. Compensation, title, perquisites, and opportunities can be contentious matters. The best way to deal with this, as proven repeatedly, is to practice open and honest communication. For compensation, start with market norms to manage expectations. People need to accept market forces if they want to be part of the leadership.

Parents should start planning for life after retirement well in advance. Succession planning needs to consider transitioning management to the next generation, as well as ownership. The latter is usually accomplished through estate planning. The former is the harder part. When thinking about succession, parents need to consider how they intend to spend the time they gain by not working. Planning should start three to five years ahead of any substantial change.

Not having an agreed-upon plan with clear expectations increases the risk that the parents don't leave. In too many cases, Dad still comes to the office every day—well into his eighties or nineties—for a few hours because he has nothing else to do. This doesn't help anyone.

Family businesses have been in existence since cave dwellers hunted together. Fortunately, they have evolved tremendously since then and are the core of our economy. These eight concepts can be a rubric for planning, managing, and evaluating a succession process.

Family Governance Is Not Business Governance

Family businesses are unique, and the way they are run differs from family to family. Each business has varying degrees of corporate governance. Formal governance structures grow as the business grows and becomes more complex. Governance processes trail business needs in most situations.

When family business owners realize they have issues they can't solve, they reach for outside help. What usually starts with the lawyer, banker, or golf buddy, evolves into an advisory board over time. If the family is active, and competent to run the business, there may be no need for outside fiduciary directors. But if non-family professionals are running the business, then the family is likely to need outside fiduciary directors to protect its interests. This is the model of the modern corporation. There is a well-known body of knowledge on managing these matters that I have addressed previously.

Family governance is different than business governance. Family governance determines how the family manages itself concerning the business. Most managers understand the basics of business governance through their everyday jobs. But if you work in a family business, it is not obvious that you should put family governance structures into place, and there may not be easy ways to learn.

Sometimes family governance does not become an issue until transitioning between generations of owners or active business participants. The founder may be worried that the following generations do not view the business in the same way she does. A family member who is not active in the day-to-day workings of the business may feel he should have an equal say in how it is run. Families must have discussions before these issues come up rather than addressing them on an ad-hoc basis.

Werner Wisdom

Sometimes family governance does not become an issue until transitioning between generations. It takes time to develop effective governance; don't wait.

A well-governed family has a written, enforced family constitution, including a code of conduct, annual family assemblies to teach the family about the business, and a family council where ownership makes business decisions. The family governance needs to interface effectively with business governance, especially if professional managers run the business.

A family constitution should provide rules on the roles, responsibilities, and rights of family members, whether they are in the business or not. It should be clear on the family values, especially regarding the business (e.g., you earn your position or get paid because of your last name). The constitution should define how business insiders and outsiders relate to the business and business decisions. Most importantly, a constitution provides consequences for unacceptable behavior.

Here is a typical table of contents for a family constitution:

- Preamble
- Family mission and values
- Roles and accountability
- Stock ownership
- Family employment
- Family business education
- Family council governance
- Code of conduct

Annual family assemblies become more important when there are many generations, and they are geographically dispersed. These gatherings should educate the family about the business and have the individuals build relationships with each other.

The family council should set policy for the family and provide direction to the board of the enterprise. The board of directors sets the policy for the business and may also make recommendations to the family council in matters concerning the business.

Werner Wisdom

Annual family assemblies become more important with
three or more generations geographically dispersed.

Most family ownership groups have a degree of dysfunction, in addition to the usual family issues. It is unusual for families to be able to figure this out alone. The family business consulting industry exists for this reason. Many highly skilled professionals can help families move through these issues. Having been on both sides of this table, I advocate families finding the right professional for their needs. It is often too hard to go it alone.

Family governance is a latent need that happens whether you address it or not. It takes time and money and does not service clients, employees, or generate profits. But if you have a family business, you implicitly choose priorities between the family and the business, and both can suffer if these issues are not addressed. If your goal is to pass the business to the next generation, then you need to determine what structures allow you to do that successfully so that the business will prosper when new people are running it.

Without Good Governance, Family Businesses Go Nuclear

To put it bluntly, proper governance does not come naturally for most private and family businesses. It requires leadership to understand that good governance protects the business and is sometimes worth the substantial time and effort required to achieve it.

Families will never be perfect. This is why the fundamental question is, "How much and what elements of governance are critical to safeguard the enterprise and guide it through an unknown future?"

As a reminder, here are some of the key points on family governance to keep in mind as you read the three case studies on the importance of good governance.

- Getting the unengaged to become engaged is critical to cohesiveness.
- Shared values are the starting point to managing conflict and effectively managing the family.
- Changing generations is often the best time to change the rules of family governance and business governance.
- Communications and conversations are the heart of family governance processes.

Three Families, Zero Good Governance

Here are a few examples of what happens when there is insufficient governance and leadership cannot cope with the consequences of their historical bias toward lower cost and less effort.

Family #1. The Food-Packaging Family

This second-generation business was stuck in the transition between generations. Mom and Dad had worked sixty to eighty hours a week for forty years to create this $60M enterprise. Their son had been running the business for eight years, allowing Dad to slow down and relax. But their son was running the business into the ground by misappropriating assets, playing favorites with staff and family members, and creating a toxic culture.

But Dad loved Mom, and Mom loved her son, so Dad couldn't do anything about it until the bank called to ask about their $7 million loan. The business was underperforming, and change was needed. At this point, the non-family CFO engaged consultants to fix the business and restore some order to the family politics. The eight family members enjoying their historic entitlement (a $100,000 a year salary and total absence from the office) had to accept the changes forced on them because they could not see that their decisions were harmful.

What Should Have Happened

The son should not have been allowed to flail for eight years. It was clear earlier that he was in the wrong job. After being moved to the right job, he excelled, and the company prospered.

The non-performing family members should have been held accountable, as were all non-family members. Once this was addressed, Mom and Dad slept better, had more money in the bank, and avoided being abused by the entitled family members for "not doing enough for them."

Family #2. The Metal Fabrications Family

Mom, Dad, two sons, and a daughter were all in the business. The kids were in their late fifties. Mom and Dad were still working at age eighty since they spent whatever savings they had on racecars and speedboats.

When Obamacare changed the rules for insurance reimbursement, that changed how their primary customers did business and reduced their margins. The financial stress became too much. The family members did not talk to each other about important issues, even though they worked together fifty hours a week. They could discuss operational details ad nauseum, but they avoided the topics of spending, compensation, and roles and responsibilities. They also failed to address past behaviors that were still causing schisms in the family. When Mom and Dad lost enough sleep and realized they couldn't avoid it any longer, they hired a family mediator to bridge the gaps in the working relationships.

What Should Have Happened

Mom and Dad should have forced the painful conversations before the industry got soft so that the business would not have had the high risk it did. Professional opinions solicited from outside the family would have made this easier.

Family #3. The Furniture Family

This third-generation business was owned fifty/fifty by two brothers. Dad did not want to pick favorites, so he split the business between them. Unfortunately, there was no tie-breaking mechanism, and they were unable to resolve differences easily, if at all. Disputes were solved by one brother acting while the other was out of the office, or the other brother would walk away from time to time.

Then, they received an unsolicited offer to buy the company with nice upside potential for executing the plan. But they couldn't decide what they wanted. It took them nine days to sign an NDA to start the discussion with the buyer. By that time, the buyer figured out that the brothers could not make decisions and walked away.

What Should Have Happened

You can love your brother, but you still need a way to resolve disputes and conflicts. A fifty/fifty partnership with no dispute resolution forces stalemates. The best documents are the ones you sign and never need to use. In this case, they needed a document with rules on how to break ties.

Good Governance Is The Glue
Holding Family Business Together

In each case, the family was dysfunctional and suffered because they did not communicate, avoided the core issues, and had no healthy governance processes to resolve disputes. Good governance deals with conflicts healthily, with guardrails to keep childish and non-productive behaviors out of the business.

As businesses grow and get more complex, the importance of good governance grows, too. That is why $10 million revenue businesses don't have boards, $30 million to $50 million revenue businesses move toward a board of advisors, and $300 million to $500 million revenue companies have difficulty functioning without a fiduciary board of directors. While true for most private companies, it is more evident when looking at family businesses. While not hard and fast rules, these observations have stood the test of time.

As we leave family businesses behind, the time has come to examine the final secret. You need to have a plan for the rest of your life, to be considered in the final chapter.

Your Ownership Journey

Secret #11. Understand How Family Businesses Are Different

» Family businesses have two difficulties compared to public companies: raising capital and attracting the best talent.

» Family businesses with more mature governance processes tend to have a more informed, deliberative decision-making process and are more likely to make consensual decisions.

» A well-governed family has a written, enforced family constitution, annual family assemblies to teach the family about the business, and a family council where ownership makes business decisions.

» Proper governance does not come naturally for most private and family businesses. It requires leadership to understand that good governance protects the family and the business.

» Good governance is about dealing with conflicts healthily, with guardrails to minimize childish and non-productive behaviors.

Plan For The Later Stages Of Life

Regardless of your end game, the goal is to have no regrets at the end of your entrepreneurial journey. The way to ensure that happens is to plan for your next stage of life before you get there.

"Many outsiders look at those who receive money from the sale of a family business as 'lucky' and 'living on easy street,'" says attorney Lauren J. Wolven. "While there is an advantage to having financial security, there is also a lot of emotional adjustment and financial education that must take place with a liquidity event."

Litigation, aimless heirs, and financial ruin are only a few of the pitfalls that must be avoided when contemplating a family business liquidity event.

"With proper planning and good advice, however, most shareholders and family business insiders can make a successful transition to the post-sale phase of their lives," adds Wolven.

After Retirement The Game Of Life Is Different

Speaking of making a successful transition, something important that I learned from my dad, Dick Werner, is the value of realizing that after retirement, life will be different—and it's necessary to create a new life. Many people identify so greatly with their jobs that they have a hard time adapting to not holding that position anymore—but we are not our jobs. We are people who need to go forward as people.

My father spent a couple of years putting the building blocks in place, so when he retired and put the keys on the table, it was a seamless transition. He is an excellent example of winning the game of life. He had a phenomenal career—was incredibly successful with a long list of accomplishments—and then he walked away from it and only got happier.

Dad turned ninety in March 2021, and he just published his first book. He has so many things to do that I have trouble keeping up with them—he still plays golf three or four times a week, plays bridge, and runs our family foundation. He's been married to his high school sweetheart for almost seventy years, is a father of three, grandfather to seven, and great-grandfather to six.

The point of sharing this is that in the end, it's not about the money—it's about happiness. It helps to have money but selling your business and getting a pile of money only to be miserable because you have no reason to get out of bed in the morning is no way to live. There are many stories of those who fall into that category and end up dying within six months.

As a business owner, you need to think ahead because one day, you're not going to work. Presumably, you're going to live longer than your work years if you're lucky.

While you can fill your time with hobbies or play golf, you also need to replace the challenges that drove you as a business owner with something else, whether it's not-for-profit work or a second career—because just leaving with nothing planned can put you in an early grave.

Don't Wait Too Long To Sell The Company

Not every business is dealt a winning hand. A board member called me on a Tuesday, informing me that the company couldn't make Thursday's payroll without a bank loan. Luckily, the loan came through on time. I was asked to submit a bid to restructure the business so the owners could delay or avoid selling the company, and fortunately, I won the assignment.

We immediately moved to reduce overhead by 40 percent. This was possible since the business model and markets had shifted to a less-intensive service model, but the company was still carrying staff from the older, high-service way of doing things. So, while it was painful to the individuals, the business was shedding unneeded functions.

Next, we negotiated with the bank to buy time and avoid selling the company. We refinanced the existing debt, spreading out the payments to ease the monthly burn. Due to a good relationship and strong prospects, the bank complied with our financing request. The core business was healthy; it just needed time to restructure.

Then, we went about rebuilding the management team and compensation structures. We added significant recruiting and marketing capabilities since that is what we needed to drive growth. Since we had cut every possible cost (including the owner taking no income), we had to grow our way out of trouble.

After twelve months of work, we had the business on a good track. The new management team had gelled, the business plan was optimistic, and the team felt good about the situation.

But at the same time, we knew the market was changing. While we were busy trying to save this business, many new competitors had entered the business. The industry was being flooded with hot, private equity money; recent deals were peaking at fifteen times EBITDA, a measurement used to compare profitability among competitors. The competitive landscape was changing. New competitors were picking off our key employees.

Our owner was also coming close to his natural retirement age. While he wanted to work for a few more years, he knew that he'd have to sell the company for a specific minimum amount to ensure his financial security.

Everyone knew the acquisition frenzy wouldn't last, but no one knew when the music would stop. There were numerous forecasts to suggest we had a year, maybe two years, maybe less. But we knew that we would only know the tide had turned in retrospect, and it would be easy to miss the market if we waited too long.

Tax Planning In Anticipation Of A Liquidity Event

By Lauren J. Wolven, JD

The process of contemplating a liquidity event generally takes at least a year and sometimes spans several years. If a family has not contemplated tax planning before the liquidity exploration process, such planning should be one of the first items on the checklist of things to accomplish. Once a company has been taken to market or an offer has been received, valuation is clear. Before the external market has been explored, however, valuation may be less certain and leveraging opportunities may be greater.

Installment sales to grantor trusts, GRATs, use of lifetime gift exclusion, and generation-skipping transfer tax exemption are all options that should be considered before or at the front end of the liquidity event process. Family limited partnerships or LLCs are also effective planning tools for transferring some of the business interests downstream, with the ability to use them limited somewhat depending on the corporate structure of the family business itself.

One other planning item to consider when a liquidity event may be in the nearer future is ownership by younger generations. I have often seen trusts set up for grandchildren of the principal owner generation before a family business spiked in value without contemplation of a liquidity event. The trust may own only 5 percent of the business interests, but if the business is sold for $50 million and the trust provides for mandatory income distributions to the beneficiary starting at age twenty-one, there may be a problem. Dealing with inappropriate or inflexible trusts is a separate topic, but for the purposes of monetizing a family business, it is important to address these issues before the liquidity event.

Contemplating The Personal Impact Of A Liquidity Event

The amount of money placed in the hands of younger generations through pre-existing estate planning structures is just one of the many personal aspects of a liquidity event that should be considered. For all family members, the impact of the new wealth can be significant. While the family may always have been wealthy on paper, having liquid wealth is different than owning valuable business interests.

Family members need to find financial advisors who can help them budget properly and understand realistic spending capabilities with the new wealth. The liquidity created from a business sale is not endless, and if not properly managed, it can lead to foreclosures and other financial difficulties. Good investment firms will help the owners define their financial goals, model their investment portfolio, and set an appropriate budget for new purchases (like a bigger home) and long-term spending. For the family members of retirement age, the ones who probably spent the better part of their lives working in and building the family business, adjusting to their new "business" of investing can be difficult, particularly in recent years. Find financial advisors willing to go slowly, educate the client, and assist the client in acclimating to a different, usually more passive, role.

For employees of the family business, there are other considerations. Time spent working in a family business is not considered a positive by all prospective employers, and the skill set of each family employee may not translate well to other business opportunities. Those employed in the family business need to consider what they will do with their lives after the liquidity event. There may be an employment contract that requires one to stay with the company during a transition period. The family may want to consider hiring career counselors to help family employees (and other employees) analyze their skills, interests, opportunities, and additional education.

Depending on the size of the deal and the family's needs, establishing a family foundation can provide a second career for some family members. For those who are younger but find themselves in a situation where they do not need to work, the lack of purpose resulting from the loss of a job at the family business can be a tremendous challenge to a relationship with one's spouse or partner, children, and in other aspects of their personal lives. Many of these individuals have found a new and satisfying purpose by taking some of their wealth and devoting themselves and this wealth to charitable causes that motivate them.

Missed Opportunity: A Failed Business Exit

In the past twenty years, there has been no significant competitors who could threaten the business. A few small shops were competitive nuisances, but no one was a mortal threat. Now, a major competitor was targeting each of our prime locations and stealing key staff.

We had fixed enough of the business to have a reasonable sale, so I recommended that the owner sell while the market was hot, but he deferred. He thought that he could get more value by spending another year improving the business further.

Another year passed, and the business was doing worse, not better. The competition got tougher. The supply chain flexed its muscle and took back a piece of the profits it didn't have before, reducing margins materially. The new management team had a few hiccups.

So, we hired an investment banker, and the sale process began. We started to hear rumors of buyers walking away from deals saying, "That is just too expensive to buy." There were already cracks in the market.

Then COVID-19 broke out, and everything got harder. Buyers walked away or reduced their bids. Eventually, the business was sold for a lower price and on less favorable terms than where the process started.

Don't wait too long to sell the company. Every day you are not selling your business, you are buying it back.

Focus On Representations, Warranties, And Indemnities, Not Just Price

Some years after the deal closes, people tend to forget how much money they made, which is okay. Life moves forward. But representations, warranties, and indemnities might last forever. These deal terms tend to impact sellers more than the price because they cannot be changed and can come back to haunt you later.

You will likely need to make representations and warranties as shareholders, separate from the company. Once you sell, no business entity pays the legal expenses for defense or prosecution of shareholder matters. That is separate from the aggravation of what was likely intended to be a blissful retirement.

So, when the lawyers are hammering out the language, pay attention.

Transactions Are A Team Sport

If you are not a dentist, would you practice dentistry at home? Probably not. The team of professionals you engage with and how they manage the process are critical to a good outcome. Even if you have not been involved in a transaction before, you need to understand the positions on the team and manage the game.

The Goal Is No Regrets

Transactions are processes, not events. While they are intended to be well-scripted, they are typically turbulent. Learning how to deal with the turbulence—managing emotions and making tough decisions under pressure—is critical. If the professionals helping you are on their game, they will actively manage information flow and expectations to keep clients focused. They need to know their clients if they are doing their job.

Many owners work their whole lives in their business and exit to move to the next phase of life. They want to feel good about their careers and legacies. They do not want to be haunted by what could have or should have happened on their watch. That is why I always ask, "What do we need to do so you have no regrets when you walk away?" This is part of the goal-setting process mentioned earlier and is often the most impactful question of all.

The goal is to have no regrets. Once you sell your business, it is time to move forward with your life.

After all, most people work to live, not live to work, so why have regrets when you are all done?

In conclusion, I wish you the best on your ownership journey.

Your Ownership Journey

Secret #12. Plan For The Later Stages Of Life

» Every day you are not selling your business, you are buying it back.

» A great deal of emotional adjustment and financial education must happen in parallel with a liquidity event.

» Litigation, aimless heirs, and financial ruin are only a few of the pitfalls that must be avoided when contemplating a family business liquidity event.

» Private company owners should examine their estate planning needs in conjunction with initiating an exit process.

» Many individuals have found a new and satisfying purpose by taking some of their wealth and devoting themselves to charitable causes that motivate them.

» The goal is to have no regrets. Once you sell your business, it is time to move forward with your life.

Chapter Takeaways

Secret #1. Why The Ownership Journey Is A Rocky Road

It's not about finding the right answers in life. It's about asking the right questions.

While most of your time is spent working *in* the business, the high-impact decisions you will make pertain to working *on* the business.

Ownership strategy defines what the owners want from the asset they own. A business strategy is what you do to get there.

Private company owners can do whatever they want, so long as they pay their taxes and their bank is happy.

When you see a company get into trouble, it is usually because management fails to adjust to market conditions.

It is easy for successful owners to get too comfortable as time marches on.

Secret #2. Ownership Strategy Comes First

Consider how owning a business will help you win the game of life.

The business is an asset, and it should be used to help you achieve your life goals.

Success is about perseverance and adapting to changes beyond your control.

Wisdom is a business issue since it has the most impact in uncertain, variable, and risky situations.

Pursuing pleasure does not always lead to happiness; for the same reason, there is often declining marginal pleasure from acquiring material possessions.

Secret #3. Business Strategy Drives Objectives, Then Tactics

Strategy was once defined as trying to gain an unfair advantage in the marketplace.

Strategy is done top-down; implementation is done bottom-up.

If you have the right plan and execute the details properly, you should get the right results.

Owners must master the five competitive forces; it only takes one to deprive you of success.

Structure follows strategy; there is always a reason why industries and businesses are structured the way they are. Is your business structured for success?

Since lost opportunities compound as the market grows, not taking enough risk can become very expensive over time.

Secret #4. Find Capital And Talent To Enable Strategy

Money is a commodity. Whether it is debt or equity, how it is structured reflects the impact of the combination of people, ideas, and opportunities.

The three steps to raising capital are: (1) set the business strategy and support it with detailed planning, (2) decide how much and the form of capital to fund the plan, and (3) demonstrate that you can be trusted to return the money with a risk-adjusted amount of profit.

Even if you find the perfect deal, you still need to be sure that you are compatible with your new partners.

In most organizations, only a few people make the critical difference between success and failure.

When you think about your leadership and management needs, consider where you want the business to be in three to five years. What will the organization chart look like then?

Effective outside directors are often the "adult in the room" to keep the business healthy and the insiders focused on the business' best interests.

Outside directors are sometimes the only force that can break a stalemate or provide the leadership to take a private company through a perilous situation.

Secret #5. Execute Organic Growth And M&A To Achieve The Strategy

A great growth strategy is useless if the leadership does not have the discipline to stay focused and execute the plan. It is important to avoid shiny object syndrome on your way to success.

There is a market for buying and selling companies, just like any other market. If you don't understand the market, take some time to get educated before betting your business.

Reward is about numbers; risk is about judgment.

Acquisitions can be exciting, but that doesn't mean they should be executed. Sometimes choosing not to act is the right decision, though inaction may feel less satisfying in the moment.

The bigger the deal's price tag, scale, and complexity, the greater need for outside perspective.

Secret #6. Assess And Develop Proper Governance

Governance is the bridge between ownership and management. It is best served by independent thinkers not distracted by personal agendas.

Board members must maintain objectivity in all circumstances; this is their primary responsibility.

Strategy and succession planning are the responsibilities

that a board manages to create value, while capital structure and risk management are more often seen as ways to protect the enterprise. Oversight is why the board is considered the "adult in the room."

While public companies are required to have boards, most private companies do not have functioning or effective boards.

Advisory boards are usually formed when critical matters are too difficult for ownership to handle on their own.

Boards of directors have fiduciary responsibilities: duty of care, loyalty, and good faith. Although like fiduciary boards, the duties of an advisory board are defined by the ownership that creates it and may be limited or non-existent.

Secret #7. Plan For Management Succession

Not making a decision is a decision, and it usually winds up being a bad one.

Succession planning is the biggest risk for most private companies.

There should be separate and parallel paths for planning management succession and ownership succession.

Proactive management succession planning is the hallmark of a well-run organization. More than thinking about who the next CEO will be, how do you develop the layers of direct reports which will be pulled up the organization chart or moved aside?

Since succession planning impacts people's careers and livelihoods, thoughtful communication is critical. Who needs to know what and when without creating a rumor mill?

A good facilitator will constructively challenge the thinking of everyone involved in succession planning.

Secret #8. Utilize Conflict Resolution And Mediation To Build Effective Relationships

Conflict can be healthy or unhealthy, but either way, it needs to be dealt with.

Identifying and managing conflict is a necessary evil for any business owner, and many tools exist to assist with that process.

Personal agendas can sometimes be negotiated. Personal values typically cannot be negotiated, except under a few extreme circumstances.

Dismissing conflict in a family enterprise as greed is too easy. More likely, stakeholders are fighting about real emotional needs, such as self-purpose and personal identity.

When the family bond does not provide enough leverage to achieve compromise or a commitment to personal change, litigation or separation might be the likely outcome.

Secret #9. Keep Getting Results

When things are bad, employees will follow leaders who

demonstrate strong character. Ultimately, this kind of leadership is what separates great companies from good companies.

Businesses that pull through crises do so because leadership has cultivated the ability to expect the unexpected.

Resilience is an absolute measure of the management team's ability to manage change and uncertainty. There is a reason people say that "it's all about the people."

If you are running a business today, you have likely lived through the October 1987 crash, 9/11, the 2008 recession, and now a global pandemic. Black swan events are a part of life, just not everyday occurrences. You should expect them.

Disaster recovery plans are associated with security breaches, fires, hurricanes, and other singular events. Business resilience is about survival and adaptation to existential problems.

Secret #10. Know How Selling A Business Works

As a business owner, you need to realize that if you know nothing about the rules of the game to sell a business, you need help.

A business is only worth what a willing buyer will pay at a point in time.

My advice to owners is to first listen to what the bankers are saying about valuation. If you don't like the pricing, do something about it because it is still your business.

Price is important, but certainty of closing becomes precious as the process moves forward. Once you are invested in the exit process, you want to get it done as quickly as possible.

Typically, terms and conditions determine long-term satisfaction with the transaction. People don't talk about the extra money they receive if they are unhappy with the outcome.

Secret #11. Understand How Family Businesses Are Different

Family businesses have two difficulties compared to public companies: raising capital and attracting the best talent.

Family businesses with more mature governance processes tend to have a more informed, deliberative decision-making process and are more likely to make consensual decisions.

A well-governed family has a written, enforced family constitution, annual family assemblies to teach the family about the business, and a family council where ownership makes business decisions.

Proper governance does not come naturally for most private and family businesses. It requires leadership to understand that good governance protects the family and the business.

Good governance is about dealing with conflicts healthily, with guardrails to minimize childish and non-productive behaviors.

Secret #12. Plan For The Later Stages Of Life

Every day you are not selling your business, you are buying it back.

A great deal of emotional adjustment and financial education must happen in parallel with a liquidity event.

Litigation, aimless heirs, and financial ruin are only a few of the pitfalls that must be avoided when contemplating a family business liquidity event.

Private company owners should examine their estate-planning needs in conjunction with initiating an exit process.

Many individuals have found a new and satisfying purpose by taking some of their wealth and devoting themselves to charitable causes that motivate them.

The goal is to have no regrets. Once you sell your business, it is time to move forward with your life.

APPENDIX B

BadgerCo Case Study

While Chandler and Porter, in Secret #3, create the mental framework for driving strategy and execution, success is still about the details. This case study, BadgerCo, was prepared by Tim McClure at Blue Oak Strategy (https://www.blueoakstrategy.com/).

It is an effective toolset for private companies to organize these thoughts and convert them into a specific, measurable, and meaningful action plan. While most owners work on mission, vision, and key imperatives, few have the time and focus on pulling it together succinctly, as presented here.

Case Study: Path To Consistent, Profitable Growth

BadgerCo is a custom fabricator of industrial process equipment. The company provides made-to-order modular systems mounted on skids or trailers to remote operating locations. BadgerCo had grown to $13 million in annual sales driven almost entirely by one large account (an OEM in the power generation industry). The revenue cycle was long, and while the custom "build to spec" nature of the work was highly profitable, projects were "lumpy" and led to dramatic swings in revenue from quarter to quarter and year to year. The president of BadgerCo was eager to break this cycle and grow sales in a more steady and predictable way.

BadgerCo engaged Blue Oak, a management consulting firm specializing in research and strategy, to facilitate the development of a multi-year strategic plan. Blue Oak chartered a planning team comprised of executives from each key department: engineering, supply chain, operations, sales and finance. Through a series of planning sessions, the team reviewed company performance, analyzed competitors, and gathered data for key end-markets. They identified the company's strengths and weaknesses, took inventory of competitive assets, and prioritized opportunities for improvement and growth. Together, the BadgerCo leadership team painted a clear picture of the company they wanted to become with a roadmap to make it happen.

There are many ways to approach strategic planning and capture the output of the process. Blue Oak utilized a *Strategic Framework* model to organize and communicate strategic goals and decisions. The Strategic Framework is structured like a book with three chapters. Each chapter answers a fundamental question: *Who are we? Where are we going? How are we going to get there?* The contents of each chapter vary based on the needs of the business. The critical, must-have components are: Mission, Vision, Key Imperatives (focus area over the life of the vision) and Key Initiatives (annual initiatives, projects, and "work to do" under each imperative). A summary of BadgerCo's strategic plan is shown below.

Having the leadership team aligned around this game plan was a breakthrough, but the plan was worthless without execution. The BadgerCo leadership team had long held a weekly staff meeting. Once a month, this meeting was re-purposed and dedicated to progress updates on the strategic plan. The team used a simple, status-at-a-glance dashboard. The point person for each initiative gave a brief progress report, focusing on execution challenges that might require a course adjustment or additional resources. These review meetings created a forum for the leadership team to give an honest assessment of progress and hold each other accountable. After a few months, the dashboard needed to be re-stocked as initiatives were completed. Wins were celebrated, lessons learned were shared, and then new projects were added to the list. Through these review meetings, the dashboard became a living document rather than a static list. Over time, the next level of leadership at the company was included in the process. Managers took a more active role in planning, sequencing, and executing initiatives. The result: better decisions, higher ownership, and a company ahead of schedule in achieving its vision.

Strategy Summary

Who are we?

> **MISSION:**
> BadgerCo supplies and supports the remote installation and service of complex industrial systems for power generation, clean tech and water filtration markets

Where are we going?

VISION 2023:

By 2023 we will achieve $50 million in net sales with EBITDA margin of over 10%.

We will:

✔ *Reduce our customer concentration*

✔ *Develop our own product designs*

✔ *Diversity end-market risk*

✔ *Expand credentials & certifications*

	Today	2023
Net Sales	$13 mil	$50 mil
Sales to OEM "X"	$10 mil	$15 mil
Water Filtration Rev	-	$5 mil+
Engineering FTEs	4	10
...		
EBITA Margin	9-11%	>10%

Who are we?   **KEY IMPERATIVES:**

Develop Standard Product Lines	Capture Revenue From Kitting & Testing Services	Diversity End Market Exposure	Expand Our Sourcing & Engineering Team

Deep Dive on Initiative Format

A. An effective initiative sets a meaningful, attainable, measurable goal

B. Defining a plan of activities is not enough: when activities are not tied to results there is a decreased likelihood that the targeted results will actually be realized

C. Defining a balanced set of measures and targeted results is not enough: The drivers of most measures are not visible; meaning every time a measure goes south, leaders must retrace their steps and determine what activities are off track

D. Leaders need to define initiatives that clearly connect activities to targeted results

- **Example: "Hire 8 additional sales people by the end of Q1 to generate $16 million in additional revenue by year end. (Owner: Tom Jones)"**

E. Each initiative should be assigned a single owner and be written to pass the "SMART" test (see boxes at right)

F. The collection of initiatives for a given year should provide a clear picture of how your company will execute its strategies for that year

G. Detailed actions plans may be required for large, complex or cross-functional initiatives

---

Single Owner Concept
The owner is not *solely* responsible for the execution of the initiative.

Often a large, cross-functional team is needed to get the job done.

The owner *is* the point person responsible for managing execution, raising flags, reporting status and making adjustments as required.

SMART Format
Initiatives should be written so that they pass the "SMART" test.

They should be:

- Specific
- Measurable
- Action-oriented
- Results-based
- Time-bound

Deep Dive on At-A-Glance Dashboard

Imperative	Status		Initiative	Start Date	Due Date	Cost ($000s)	Owner	Support Team
I. Increase market share		A.	Hire 8 additional sales people by the end of Q1 to generate $16 million in additional revenue by year end	Jan 1	Dec 31	$1,000	T. Jones	HR
		B.						
		C.						
II. Imperative ...		A.						
		B.						
III. Imperative ...		A.						
		B.						
		C.						
		D.						

A. A one-page dashboard is an effective tool for tracking initiatives

B. Fields in the dash can be customized to fit your business needs but should include

- Initiative
- State and due dates
- Cost
- Owner & Support Team
- Status: Darker-Lighter-Medium Gray

C. The senior leadership team should review the dashboard on a regular basis (at least quarterly, often monthly)

D. Discussion time should be focused on items that are stalled or off track (darker or lighter gray) so that decisions to adjust course or allocate additional/different resources can be made

Your Ownership Journey

Takeaways from the Case Study

» Sustained success requires a compelling strategy to provide context for execution.

» The "Strategic Framework" clearly describes who you are (Mission), where you are going (Vision) and how you are going to get there (Key Imperatives & Supporting Key Initiatives)

» An initiative defines a corporate priority and establishes a commitment to execute.

» Engaging the "next level of leaders" can improve the quality of the plan and build front-line ownership.

» Regular progress management (reviewing status, adjusting course, shifting resources) keeps the plan relevant and improves odds of success.

» Less is more: accomplishing a few critical priorities year after year is more effective than creating long lists of priorities and accomplishing few of them.

Acknowledgments

I want to thank my publisher and editors at Indie Books International: Henry DeVries, Devin DeVries, Adrienne Moch, Taylor Graham, and art director Bill Ramsey.

I have had three stages of my career: academic, family business, and entrepreneurial. Each phase has contributed to this book, and I want to express gratitude to those who have helped me to grow and learn at each phase.

I went to engineering school since it was a requirement for entry into the family business, but I didn't want to be a practicing engineer. My professors taught me how to think, solve problems, and find practical solutions to impractical problems. Thanks to Paul Wright, Ed Rubin, Warren Hausman, Charlie Fine, and the many other mentors who helped me understand how little I knew.

Working at Werner Co, even though I was an owner, was the perfect laboratory for understanding how to get things done, with real people constrained by everyday workplace issues. In addition to our family leaders, Dan Butler, Dick Sulecki, Mike Isacco, Tom Ellis, and Don Resnick deserve mention, with others too numerous to list here.

I have started four businesses; each had its own cast of characters. Two were successful, the others, not so much. I am now glad that my first start-up failed, as it taught me what business school never could.

Thank you to my clients, referral sources, business partners, and investors for providing opportunities to impact the world.

But most of all, thank you to my family for supporting me in all my endeavors.

APPENDIX D

About The Author

Bruce Werner spent the first half of his career at Werner Ladder, with executive responsibilities in all facets of the business. During that time, the family completed six acquisitions and sustained 10 percent annual growth for over a decade. The family later exited the business in a successful LBO.

As an independent consultant, he helps owners address their governance, strategy, capital, talent, and succession issues. This work is based on several decades of deep operational experience. He has started and built businesses in finance, energy, retail, and technology, in addition to being a partner in a private equity fund.

Werner has a specialty in working with family businesses, both as an advisor and as a board member. His governance experience includes forming new boards and serving on established boards, both advisory and fiduciary. He has performed audit, governance, and compensation committee work.

In the non-profit world, Werner has served as board chair and worked on governance, nominating, strategy, compensation, finance, and investment committees.

An accomplished public speaker, he has connected with business audiences across the country on these same topics, working with Bank of America Private Bank, Vistage International, Cavendish Global Forum, National Association of Home Builders, and the Turnaround Management Association. His academic relationships include Northwestern's Kellogg School, Cornell's Smith Family Business Initiative, and Loyola University's Family Business Center.

In addition to numerous webinars and podcasts, he has been published in the *Wall Street Journal, Private Company Director, Wealth Management, Estate Planning, Trusts & Estates*, and other national publications.

Werner received a BS in mechanical engineering/public policy from Carnegie-Mellon University. As an IBM Fellow, he graduated from Stanford University with an MS in manufacturing systems engineering. He completed his education at the MIT Sloan School, earning an MS management degree focusing on strategy and operations.

To contact him, send an email to bruce@konaadvisors.com. Visit his website at www.konaadvisors.com or his profile at https://www.linkedin.com/in/brucedwerner/.

Works Referenced

[1] Joshua Piven. *The Worst-Case Scenario Survival Handbook* (20th anniversary edition). San Francisco: Chronicle Books, 2019.

[2] Darrin McMahon. *Happiness: A History*. New York: Grove Press, 2006.

[3] Jan Ott. "The Measurement and Explanation of Happiness." *Beyond Economics*. December 13, 2020.

[4] Erik H. Erikson. *Identity and the Life Cycle*. New York: W. W. Norton, 1994.

[5] L. Verschaffel, B. Greer, and e. De Corte. *Making Sense of Word Problems*. United Kingdom: Taylor & Francis, 2000.

[6] Michael E. Porter. "How Competitive Forces Shape Strategy," *Harvard Business Review*, May 1979 (Vol. 57, No. 2).

[7] Alfred Chandler. *Strategy and Structure: Chapters in the History of the Industrial Enterprise*. Cambridge: MIT Press, 1962.

[8] Spencer E. Ante. *Creative Capital: Georges Doriot and the Birth of Venture Capital*. Cambridge: Harvard Business Review Press, 2008.

[9] "Understanding the Capital Stack and How It Affects Your Investments." JRW Investments. https://www.jrw.com/articles/investment-principles/understanding-the-capital-stack-and-how-it-affects-your-investments/. Feb. 14, 2013.

[10] "QCA 2020 Non-Executive Director Survey." Quoted Companies Alliance. https://www.theqca.com/article_assets/articledir_406/203371/QCA_Non-Executive_Directors_Survey_2020.pdf.

[11] "Summer 2021 Fortune/Deloitte CEO Survey." https://www2.deloitte.com/us/en/pages/chief-executive-officer/articles/ceo-survey.html.

[12] Claudio Fernández-Aráoz, Gregory Nagel, and Carrie Green. "The High Cost of Poor Succession Planning." *Harvard Business Review*, May-June 2020.

[13] "Facebook survey finds almost one-third of small businesses have stopped operating in the pandemic." MarketWatch.com, May 19, 2020. https://www.marketwatch.com/story/facebook-survey-finds-almost-one-third-of-small-businesses-have-stopped-operating-in-the-pandemic-2020-05-19.

[14] Daniel Kline. "Most Small Business Owners Lack A Succession Plan." The Motley Fool, Aug. 2, 2018. https://www.fool.com/careers/2018/08/03/most-small-business-owners-lack-a-succession-plan.aspx.

[15] Michael Gerber. *The E-Myth Revisited: Why Most Small Businesses Don't Work and What to Do About It*. New York: Harper Business, 2004.

[16] Doug Baumoel. "Getting a grip on conflict." *Family Business*, Winter 2012. https://www.familybusinessmagazine.com/sites/default/files/articles/2015/10/01/20Gettingagriponconflict Winter2012.html.

[17] All stories and case studies in this book are based on true stories, but names and some details have been changed to protect confidentiality. These stories are included for educational purposes to help business leaders better understand the points being made.

[18] Inspired by Spertus Institute for Jewish Learning and Leadership, where I serve as a member of the board of trustees. https://www.spertus.edu/news/teaching-resilence.

[19] "Hiring An Investment Bank That Specializes In M&A Improves Seller Outcomes, Here's Why." https://jdmerit.com/education/hiring-an-investment-bank/.

[20] John Davis. "How three circles changed the way we understand family business." *Family Business*. September/October 2019.

[21] KPMG. "2019 Global Family Business Survey." https://assets.kpmg/content/dam/kpmg/sa/pdf/2020/step-2019-global-family-business-survey-report.pdf.

APPENDIX F

Index